THE 'I Can' METHOD

THE
ICAN
METHOD™

Giving you strength to soar

Published in the UK in 2022 by Silver Lough Publishing

Paperback ISBN 978-1-7392100-0-7
eBook ISBN 978-1-7392100-1-4

Cover design and typeset by SpiffingCovers.com

THE 'I Can' METHOD

SARAH PITTENDRIGH

THE
ICAN
METHOD™

Giving you strength to soar

Preface by Eleanor Mills

When Sarah Pittendrigh first reached out to me to ask if I could help her write her memoir, I immediately liked the cut of her jib. She was bright, direct, funny and focused, and we hit it off on our first Zoom. Her mission to help midlife women (I like to call them Queenagers) work through the self-limiting beliefs that can hold them back chimed with my own purpose in founding a new media platform for women in midlife.

Sarah and I both believe in changing the narrative about the later stages of women's lives to one more optimistic and fit for purpose. In my 25 years at the top of the British media, as an award-winning editor at the Sunday Times and as Chair of Women in Journalism UK, I grew tired of the prevailing cultural view that women are like peaches (one wrinkle and we are done), while men are viewed like fine wine (improving with age). That is of course nonsense, but it is perfidious nonsense which gets inside women's souls and too often makes them feel diminished and insecure.

In the hundred-year-life, which many of us should be lucky enough to live, fifty is only halfway through; it is why I called my platform Noon.org.uk. In my community of Queenagers, we have a motto: So Much More to Come. I loved Sarah's mantra of Formidable Over Forty: You are Never too Old and it is Never too Late. She and I come from very different worlds (London and Northumberland), but we are firmly on the same page when it comes to re-writing the script of women's lives.

There is so much we can do to change this stubborn narrative, and books like this one which demonstrate the agency, industry and vitality of midlife women are part of the revolution. We need to tell different stories, and most importantly get them out there in the culture, so women don't feel invisible or despairing when they hit fifty, but instead feel excited about all that is ahead. I firmly believe that midlife is when women come into their prime, when we become the women we are supposed to be.

That is why I am so honoured to have helped Sarah write this book. As you will see when you read it, it is her book— her voice, her story, her thinking. She is wonderfully wise, frank—sometimes bracingly so—but also compassionate and empathetic. I also highly recommend her coaching; I was supposed to be in Northumberland to help her write this book, and my job was to interview her; but over dinner she identified my own self-limiting beliefs and encouraged me to change my business model. I followed her advice, and my revenues were transformed!

If you are a woman—or indeed a man—who is struggling to see a way forward, whether in business, or in your personal life, then this book is exactly the medicine you need.

Sarah Pittendrigh is an inspirational woman. Her story of rags to riches to bankruptcy to reinvention and triumph is the stuff that modern fairy tales are made of.

I am proud to call her my friend and wish her all love and success with her 'boook'. Give it a chance and her I CAN Method will change your life too.

Eleanor Mills

September 2022

Hello, I am Sarah Pittendrigh. I'm a successful businesswoman, a multi award-winning entrepreneur, a motivational speaker and an inspirational mentor to ambitious midlife female entrepreneurs.

Life hasn't always been this good. In fact it took me until I was in my 40s to learn how to live a life I love. Indeed, in my 50 years I feel like I have seen it all! I have been through some wonderful highs and some very dark lows. At one point I lost everything, I was at rock bottom, emotionally, mentally and financially. I was a single mum, was declared bankrupt and the bank arrived to repossess my home.

I was broken.

In this book I want to tell you my story; to share with you how I picked myself up, worked out a plan from my dining room table and created a multi award-winning company.

I transformed my life, and you can too.

I know this is true because I didn't do this by being bullet-proof or a super woman, but by working through a series of logical steps to turn everything around. It is a system that I have called The I CAN Method.

I know it works; I was the first customer, and my life story is the proof.

I hope that by telling you what happened to me truthfully, the vulnerabilities that stalked me and the dark times I endured I can inspire you to break through the challenges you are facing in your life, or business.

Many of the most successful people I've met have a kernel of self-doubt rumbling deep inside them. It is why they push so hard, never give up, always give that little bit extra; they always feel they have something to prove.

Why? Where does that feeling come from? We have to dig deep to make sense of it all. I have found it essential to go back to when we were first told we weren't good enough; to understand what sparked that sense of lack and gave us that self-limiting belief.

But after a while the drive to prove yourself can also become a curse. There is no stop button, no sense of 'I have enough'.

So many of my clients come to me saying: "I've ticked all the boxes, made lots of money, created my six or seven-figure business, but I'm still not happy. In fact, in some ways I am more unhappy because I thought when I'd got all the nice things, was successful on paper, had made it, that everything would feel okay. That I would be happy".

But the reality for so many of them when they come to see me is that they don't feel happy. They are far from okay. They are lonely. They feel their work or business controls them, that they have created a monster. "I can't feel any joy, I'm overwhelmed. I'm lonely and isolated," a top female founder told me last week.

She was so not the only one. Often these people who look like they have it all from the outside—the designer bag, the nice car, the house straight out of a magazine—don't want to admit it isn't working out so well on the inside. They are so exhausted from pretending they have it all under control that when they come to me, either in person or over video call, they break down. They often cry. It is like turning on a release valve; the tears come flooding out.

They are so relieved to finally admit what is really going on for them, to get the weight of their worries out in the open. It is a relief to them that I understand, that I get it.

They feel safe because they know that I have been there and am offering a confidential space for them to show their vulnerability, to finally offload. And it is only with that letting down of the wall, the relief of admitting that it has all got too much, that together we can begin to find the answers to the big questions.

You see, I am not surprised by their reactions or their story. I expect it. I know it goes with the territory.

But the good news is that this is fixable.

You *can* be happy. You can make a success of your life. You can have it all.

It is never too late, and you are never too old to design a life you love!

Chapter One

Growing up — ponies, bullies, and not being good enough

I was only seven when I first felt out of control, when terror first hit me. I had gone out for a ride with two children, a brother and sister who were a little older than me. Our ride would take us into a large open stubble field, with corn that had been freshly harvested, leaving behind stiff stalks that crackled under your feet. Before I had a chance to ask which way we were going, they set off into a flat-out gallop on their ponies and left me behind.

I come from Northumberland in northern England, where the skies are huge and the land stretches far to the horizon. My pony got the wind under her tail and bolted off after the others, across an open space that felt like never-ending miles to my seven-year-old self.

I was hauling on the reins, desperate to retain control, but the smooth leather kept slipping through my fingers. The pony was bucking with its head between its knees and with all my might I couldn't stop her. I was sure I was going to fall off. I was doing everything to keep my balance. I was shouting, "Stop! Please stop!" but the others just laughed at me. They thought it was really, really funny.

But I was scared—so scared. It went on for what seemed like an age and when I stopped, eventually, I was a wreck. My hands and arms were aching. My legs were like jelly. I could hardly breathe. I had suffered a real fright, and felt so out of control, but I couldn't admit it. In front of those big kids, I had to pretend everything was OK and that I wasn't really bothered. I wasn't going to show them how I really felt. I would hide my fear.

And that was my first experience of feeling out of control. The first experience of masking my anxiety behind a broad smile.

Horses are and have always been a huge part of my family life; my parents enjoyed horse racing and producing in-hand show ponies. Before mum was married, she had worked with racehorses in the UK and carriage horses in Belgium. Horses are in our blood.

We moved to a run-down farmhouse in need of a full renovation, but with its own piece of land, when I was 11, so we could keep our horses and ponies at home. It was tough in the beginning. My parents stretched themselves to buy the property. My mum and dad did much of the renovation themselves to save money. My dad would spend weekends and evenings after work on the house, ripping out walls, floors and ceilings. My mum would get my brother and I off to school and continue where my dad had left off. She was often to be seen wheeling heavy barrowloads of stone and rubble to the tip outside in all weathers. We lived in the farmhouse throughout the rebuild. I can remember having a bath in the middle of winter when there was no roof on the bathroom. There would often be more ice on the inside of the windows than out!

My parents worked hard and often tempers frayed under the pressure. I missed my grandparents, who had always lived nearby before, and my good friends from primary school.

When we first turned up at our new farmhouse, my brother and I went off to explore our surroundings. Nothing prepared us for the greeting from the local kids; they threw stones at us. It was a mark of what was to come; I was terrified of starting my new school. Rightly as it turned out. I was bullied from the day I started there. I don't really know why. A group of older girls decided that they didn't like me and made my life hell, with jeering comments, name-calling and intimidation from the very first day. I felt anxious all the time at that school. They thought I was rich because I had a pony, but that was simply not true. I certainly wasn't a privileged child.

Then the terror hit me again. I must have been 12. I had been riding a new pony in our field, who was bigger than my naughty little 12hh Welsh pony and much sharper. This new mount was a 13.2hh chestnut mare; she was hot when we finished her exercise, so mum suggested I walk her down the road to cool her down. I set off, but I hadn't gone very far when a group of horses who were turned loose in a big field next to the road began to gallop flat out. All I could hear was the stampeding of hooves over the hedge. I'll never forget those huge horses putting their noses over the hedge, running back and forth, and my pony quivering with fright. She literally spun on her heels and took off with me. She galloped away, right up the middle of the road. I was standing up in my stirrups, pulling with all my might. I thought I was going to die; I couldn't stop for love nor money. The pony was running in blind panic.

Then to my relief I saw my mum walk out across the road. I screamed for her to help me. She frantically waved her arms and luckily the pony stopped, skidding to a halt right in front of her.

I was shaking. I was terrified. But horsey people are supposed to be tough. From when you first learn to ride you are told to get straight back on the horse when you fall off, not to let the fear sink in. So, I bottled it up and didn't make too much fuss. I got on with it, but boy was I glad to feel the ground under my small feet.

That has been a pattern for me, feeling absolutely terrified but doing "it" anyway. I was never a confident rider after that. In fact, writing about those two experiences with my ponies still gives me a knot of anxiety in my stomach, and reliving it made me cry. I feel very sad for the little girl I was; she really wanted to ride, but those instances of terror—along with some nasty falls—had taken all joy out of it.

I know those two experiences were formative for me. It was where the rot started to set in. When I first truly felt I had lost confidence. They were my first experiences of a lack of self-belief.

And it was all tied up with other complicated emotions. We weren't rich, even though I got bullied for having a pony. The truth is that the ponies we had were a bit tricky; needed training. We didn't have the money for beautifully schooled, well-educated ponies. We couldn't afford them at that time.

I wasn't confident and I really would have benefitted from a pony which was a bit more forgiving, but my parents got me the best they could afford at that time.

In our family horses weren't really about fun, we weren't happy hackers; riding for us was more about competing. My parents had in-hand show ponies and I had my show pony. My father liked to win. He was competitive. My fear was amplified by a combination of naughty ponies and the pressure to perform in the ring. Since I was tiny I knew I wasn't going in there to enjoy myself. I was there to do a job. I was expected to do my best and aim to win. If I didn't, I felt I'd let them down. I was only young, but there was a definite pressure.

My father had one very good pony. His name was Rosevean Grey Owl. He had owned him from a foal. He'd showed the pony all over the country in-hand, where he had won many classes. And then when he was three, Grey Owl was sent away to be broken in.

The family who taught him to wear a saddle and bridle, and how to be ridden (we call it producing a horse), did a great job. First their older daughter rode him and then their son. Rosevean Grey Owl qualified and was placed at the Horse of the Year Show and the Royal International Horse Show; two highly prestigious events on the equine calendar.

But it really rankled with me that I wasn't the one who got to ride him. I spent many weekends on the sidelines watching the other children enjoying their success, with my dad buying them gifts to celebrate their wins and their hard work. I remember feeling so sad, wishing it was me. Even typing that sentence, remembering how much it hurt, has brought tears to my eyes. I knew that that special, beautifully trained pony was the answer to my dreams, and would have been the perfect schoolmaster for me. I remember one day they let me have a ride on him and he was the nicest pony I had ever sat on. I had a grin from ear to ear. I was excited and hopeful of having the chance to compete on him.

However, my parents were unable to let me ride him and continue the winning streak as they had to sell him. They needed the money for new windows for the farmhouse. But I was so upset. My little heart was broken. I didn't understand, I was too young, I took it so personally, and it felt like such a rejection. I felt deep inside me that I wasn't good enough. Not a good enough rider, not worthy of the ride. I can still remember sitting on the trailer of the new owners when they came to collect Rosevean Grey Owl, weeping to him as they all sat inside handing the money over. I was inconsolable. I didn't understand about windows, I just wanted a chance to be up there with the "successful kids" and to have pride in calling this beautiful pony my own.

It's strange now, looking back at the experiences that shape you. Just thinking about it, I recoil at how torn up I was. The hurt went deep. It had a terrible long-term impact in terms of my self-belief. I knew even then that that pony was my chance to conquer my fear and to gain some self-confidence, but my mum and dad needed the windows.

Now I am a mum myself, I know I wouldn't have made that decision lightly. I'd have tried to come up with other ways to get the windows and given my son a chance to chase and realise his dreams and ambitions.

And I'm not just saying that. In fact, that is exactly what I have done. My son, William, is the pride and joy of my life. He's now a professional equestrian, with many prestigious awards behind him, and his father and I have done everything in our power to help him realise his dreams. Probably because of my own experiences.

I don't blame my mum and dad. I love them both. These days we all still live near each other; in fact, the farmhouse and stable yard they built is where William keeps his horses. They are both very supportive of him and have played a big part in his life. But things were different back then. They didn't sell Rosevean Grey Owl intentionally to hurt me. They just never considered the impact. I'm sure it never entered their heads.

But the torture of that twisted inside me for years. The idea that I wasn't good enough for that pony—and most importantly for my parents—but the boy who they'd chosen to ride him instead, was. That rejection was one of the big roots of my self-limiting beliefs. That child's-eye view stuck with me.

A mixture of the fear and the rejection finished me with horses for a long time. And every time something big was going down in my life that same feeling in the pit of my stomach would pop up, as if to remind me of something massive and unresolved. I carried that deep sense of lack, of not being good enough, for a very long time.

Chapter Two

Home and family life —
how that shaped me

I'm the eldest child, and then there is my brother, who is nearly six years younger. We are very close.

I was born in Hexham, an old market town in Northumberland, and for the first 11 years of my life I lived in a small, picturesque village not far from there called Ovington. It was a community where everyone knew everyone, and it had the added benefit of my mother's family living in the neighbouring village of Ovingham. My great-grandmother was born at the village farm. And then, when I was 11, we moved to the small hamlet where I still live now, on the County Durham/Northumberland border.

My father was an Agricultural Advisor and my mum looked after my brother and I full-time.

The first house we lived in was a 16th-century brewery cottage steeped in history. Mum and dad rented it when they were first married, and later when the opportunity came around, they bought it. The property required a huge amount of work—it was terribly run down and very outdated. Together they worked tirelessly to more-or-less rebuild it. The cottage was beautiful when they finished, but the renovation had really taken its toll on them both. They were exhausted. Sympathetically restored to retain many original features—including low ceilings, traditional beams and open stone fireplaces—I loved it. I loved living there. It felt like home, not just a house.

Probably because my parents had so much work to do, I used to spend a lot of time with my granny and grandad. Not that I would complain. I loved being with them, and I called them Minnie and Grandad. I'd go and stay with them nearly every Friday after school, through till Sunday night if I could. We were so close. They would spoil me as grandparents often like to do. We'd go on holiday every summer—a caravan or cottage kind of holiday. I have such happy memories from our time together in the Mumbles in Wales and Cornwall to name just two. I loved singing as a child (to be honest I still do). Every Friday evening I would join my granny at choir practice in the local village hall, and I'd sing with her every Sunday evening in the church choir too. It was very cosy being with them.

If I'm honest, sometimes home was challenging when I was a little girl. There was a lot of pressure due to doing up the cottage while living there, especially with dad working and mum also juggling young children, along with keeping the competition ponies and their horses.

When I was 11 it was announced that we were moving. My parents had bought the farmhouse and we moved to where they still live now. Oh, how I cried. I so did not want to move, especially away from my family and friends and certainly not to another cold, ramshackle, old-fashioned, rundown house that was to be a bigger renovation project than the one my parents had just completed. Because of the state of the house, it reflected in the price, and that was how mum and dad were able to purchase it. Dad was excited because it had its own land and was set in beautiful countryside with far-reaching views. Before that they'd had to rent fields and stables for their horses off other people, so it was a dream come true for them. But it certainly came with a big financial pressure at a time when interest rates were crazy. They went up to 16% at one time when mum and dad had really borrowed a large sum of money. So the pressure was on to complete the work as quickly as possible. I know my dad really felt it. Both of them drove themselves very hard, working night and day.

Often at breakfast time there would be a meeting to discuss the work to be done on the house that day. Dad would go off to work, saying "I need the plaster off this wall today" and Mum would be chipping plaster off the old walls and shovelling it into wheelbarrows, pushing it to the tip. As if she didn't have enough to do. She was supporting and caring for her grandparents, her parents and her young children, as well as cooking a meal for dad coming home. She also had a small flock of sheep! And I suppose dad was going off to work knowing he was coming back to face what had become another job. It didn't make for a relaxed and happy atmosphere!

I suppose what I'm getting at is that it was a stressful environment to live in when I was growing up. I often felt I was walking on eggshells, like something might blow. It was a tense and pressured environment. Tempers often frayed. It made me anxious. I was a nervous child, and I kept a lot to myself. I didn't want to bother people, particularly my parents, as I didn't want to cause them any more problems, and they had enough to worry about. So I kept a lot of my own worries to myself, which ultimately would make me more anxious. I'd bottle it all up, but I always had a smile on my face, even when I was feeling miserable

I think that's why those past incidents with the tricky ponies and being so out of control were so pivotal. Because they came against a backdrop of family stress, the big house move and then the troubles that came with the new school. It was all such an anxious, uncertain time and I didn't always have my grandparents to rely on.

My early teenage years were, in a nutshell, dreadful. I'd felt so secure in the knowledge that my grandad and Minnie and their parents were living so close to me before the big move. I saw them most days. I could walk to their house from school. Even though we only moved 12 miles away it felt like a new world, and not one I enjoyed. I would only see my grandparents at weekends, and it felt like I'd been wrenched away from everyone and everything I knew and loved. I became very insecure.

Here I was with the kids throwing stones when we arrived, and then the bullying at the new school by the older girls. It just began as soon as I arrived. I have no idea why. They decided from the first day I started that new school that I was not welcome, I couldn't fit in, and it wasn't for the sake of trying. I did make friends with a couple of girls from my year and that was nice. But I'd be terrified walking around or going to their house after school for tea because the core of the bullies lived in their village. They were older girls; 12 or 13 to my 11. They just decided they didn't like my face. The new girl was not welcome and that was it, nothing was going to change their minds, so I was anxious all the time at school and anxious most of the time at home. It was a complicated time. But it is important to share this as I know I am not the only one; I know my experience will resonate with others.

As I got older, things improved. Over time, I became good friends with some of the boys from the farms nearby. I was a bit of a tomboy, certainly not a girly girl. Ironically some of the boys who had thrown stones at me and my brother when we arrived became my mates. We would hang out on our bikes and ultimately had a nice little gang. But school was never comfortable. I was very, very anxious. I hated that school and counted down the days until I left.

Luckily, I only had to stick it out for two years and then I started High School. It was a bigger space and I could avoid the bullies. They mellowed too, and eventually left me alone. Some even became quite pleasant. I made new friends, secure, longer-term friends, including one girl who was very like-minded to me. She also had a horse, and we became such good friends.

This was the first time I had experienced the feeling of having a best friend. But there was still a hangover from the bullying. A pattern of anxiety. I would dread having to talk in class, and if I was ever asked to stand in front of everyone to do a talk I would physically shake. I do believe that sense of panic grew from leaving my safe extended-family world, from the terror with the ponies and then being bullied and not being able to share any of that with my parents because I knew they were already stressed. I would say I have always quietly carried anxiety.

One of the things that helped alleviate those anxious feelings was sport. I loved playing sport. I was a good netball player, hockey player and tennis player. I just loved any sport (except cross-country running!). Being on the teams at the high school—goal attack and a goal shooter in netball. right inner, left inner for hockey—made me popular. I was always the one who was driving forward into the goal, the one who would push through. Even though I was anxious, I was always competitive. We all are in my family: my dad with the horses and his rugby, and my brother, who was a very good rugby player, playing at county level. As a family we really do like to win. We don't do something with the intention of being runner-up. You know, it was always considered that "second is first of the losers". We were always encouraged to do our best and go all out for the win.

Being pushed to win but also being anxious wasn't a good mix. The way I dealt with emotion was by learning how to put my purpose ahead of my fear. If I unravel that, what I mean is when I am terrified, I always try to think of the end goal and why it means so much to me. And I push through and make myself do it, despite the feeling of fear. Feel the fear and do it anyway! My mantra has always been 'just do it'. And when it came to sport, weirdly I didn't feel anxious, I felt confident and in control. I think I was less anxious if I was part of a team. I was more scared if it was drama or singing, especially if I had to go on stage.

I remember being offered the place of Nancy in a school production of *Oliver*. I was so thrilled to have been offered the role, but terrified about performing. I did it though; I would push myself through the fear. It was a mindset of "this feels terribly uncomfortable, I am terrified, but it would feel so much worse not to do it and miss the opportunity". Given the family pressure to achieve, I couldn't just sit on the side and look in. It was unthinkable. So I would pluck up the courage and have a go. I was always so glad that I did, even if it was painful at the time. I was proud of myself for getting through. I think that pushing through fear is something very innate in me. It didn't come from my parents. They didn't know how fearful I was as I never really shared my feelings. But when I did, my mum would always be supportive, saying I could do it and to give it my best shot. It's funny that thinking about her being like that now makes me really emotional. My dad was the one who just wanted me to win, whatever the cost. I knew if I didn't win he would be disappointed. And if I didn't win that time, he would be expecting me to do better the next time. Whereas my mum would encourage me to win for me and would still be supportive even if I didn't.

That strange mixture of anxiety and grit are the origins of my determination and steeliness. I just wanted to make my parents proud. But I think the hunger for approval which I have always felt is because when I didn't do well, I could physically FEEL my dad's disappointment. And that was hard. He always felt I could do better, and that was a hard thing to live with. Those very high standards around me made for a pressured environment. I just felt like my dad, my school, everyone around me was saying "could do better". In fact, my school reports invariably ended, "could do better", when all of the time I thought I was doing my best. It demotivated me. I needed the carrot, not the stick!

Looking back now I think all that trying too hard put me under a lot of strain, and certainly contributed to me struggling at school. That constant feeling of "could do better" undermined my confidence.

I didn't like the education system. I felt like I was being controlled, rather than supported. I think it reminded me of the feeling of being very controlled by my dad's high standards when I was younger. Then when I felt controlled by school, I hated it. I felt choked, I craved to be independent. I saw making money as a way of taking control of my life, a way to escape. I discovered that if I had money I could buy what I wanted, do what I wanted and go where I wanted. It also meant that my dad couldn't control my every move. So, from the age of 15 I started working and paying my own way. I had a holiday job and would work as often as I could when I wasn't at school. Making money was my ticket to freedom.

At 15 I was picking strawberries at the local strawberry farm. Mum used to take me down at five o'clock in the morning; I'd toil away at it all day, picking endless trays of them. Then I got promoted to the packing shed! I also worked in the local pub at weekends. Then I started work with a large supermarket chain and would do two evenings on the tills and one as a shelf stacker. I worked for them from when I turned 16 all through sixth form and college until I was 19. That job meant I could put petrol in my own car, buy clothes, or whatever. Having my own money gave me a sense of control, and I liked it.

I always felt that money brought me freedom. I didn't have to ask anyone for anything. I rarely asked my parents for money, and my grandparents gave me pocket money whenever I went back to see them. Even as a teenager they looked after me; going back to their village always felt like going home

But while I had a measure of financial freedom, I was stymied from doing what I really wanted, which was to study equestrianism at the Warwickshire College of Agriculture. My GCSEs weren't good enough for A levels, which I would never have wanted to do anyway. Horses were my passion and I really wanted to be an Equestrian Coach. But Dad didn't want me to do that; he wanted me to get a "proper" job and just see horses as a hobby.

I remember after my GCSEs we had a career appointment, and this teacher guy said "The best we could hope for is that Sarah could be a secretary". Today that feels so wrong. But back then I believed him, and off I went to do business and secretarial studies: RSA typing, shorthand, all of that malarkey. Dad really pushed me to get in to sixth form to do a BTEC in business and finance. I wasn't that keen, but I did it, and passed with distinctions and merits. That got me to the local Durham College, where I did a diploma in Business Studies, and afterwards to a postgraduate programme in management at Durham University Business School. I found all of this very boring, but believed it was what needed to be done in order to get a "proper" job!

Things got better as I got older. I loved being in the pub with all the locals on a Saturday night, where I worked with a bunch of lovely older ladies behind the bar. I've always respected people I worked with, and I've always thought that everybody's an important cog in a wheel, that it doesn't matter what sort of level or what job you're doing. We're all just trying to make a living, aren't we?

So yes, I was still anxious, but the outside world saw a vibrant, blonde, smiley, happy-go-lucky girl. Of course, that wasn't a true reflection; I had a much darker side which nobody saw. I looked bright and cheerful, but the reality was I had no confidence whatsoever and was full of self-limiting beliefs. I was haunted by the bullying, feeling that I didn't fit, feeling controlled, out of control and not able to really do what I wanted. I just felt I wasn't good enough, ever, and lived in a permanent state of anxiety. Living a life to please other people.

Chapter Three

First marriage and a breakdown

I got married when I was 23. Looking back now that seems ever so young. Stewart and I had known each other since we were tiny little children. I used to get his hand-me-downs, jodhpurs and riding hats; that was the sort of friendship we had. He's nearly a year older than me. As children we spent many weekends competing against each other on our ponies and generally hanging out at horse shows. Our parents were also friends, so we would often go around to each other's houses to play. We started going out together when we were about 19.

Stewart was an only child. His parents owned a small farm in Northumberland and had a retail milk business. Their main passion was horses. They produced and competed show horses and then, when Stewart turned 16—old enough to hold an amateur jockey's licence—they turned their attention to National Hunt racing and Point-to-Pointing.

I hadn't seen Stewart for a year—he'd been away in Ireland where he had been working with racehorses—when we bumped into each other again one night in a local pub.

It was great to catch up and we started going out with each other. Unfortunately, Stewart's parents were not as happy as we were. They didn't think I was good enough for him. They made it very clear that they wanted him to marry a farmer's daughter, preferably someone with land and more opportunity for their son than they believed I could offer. Someone a lot smarter and richer than me. How do I know? They told me, and anyone else who would listen.

This made it really hard for me. It hit all my most sensitive spots—that they didn't think I was good enough, and that they didn't want me and Stewart to be together. It really hurt.

I remember one particularly painful incident when Stewart was riding at Southwell races. He was my boyfriend and I wanted to support him, so I would try whenever I could to be there to watch him and video his events. When you go racing it is an opportunity to get all dressed up, and I always tried to make an effort to look nice for Stewart. I'd been staying with Minnie and grandad the night before, got up early, put on my smart clothes and set off to drive down to his farm. I was so looking forward to our day out and watching him ride.

I walked into the farm kitchen and there was his father sitting in "his" chair. He looked me up and down and then said: "Sorry, you can't come racing with us today. There's no room in the car. Stewart is taking me".

I was so shocked and embarrassed that I didn't know what to say. These days I'd tell him to naff off and stay at home himself. But back then I was anxious, insecure, and didn't have the self-belief or strength. The worst thing was that I remember looking at Stewart, desperately wanting him to stand up for me. To say to his dad, "No, she's coming with us!" But he feared his father. He never argued with him, and he just went along with that.

I took a deep breath, contained my tears, and left.

I walked out of that kitchen and got back into my car, the pain stabbing my stomach. I cried all of the way home, back to my granny. I felt not only heartbroken but like a worthless reject.

That wasn't the only time Stewart's parents treated me badly. I remember one day ringing the farmhouse and Stewart's father answering the phone. When I asked if Stewart was available, he not only said he wasn't, but added nastily: "Don't ring this house. Ever. If Stewart wants to speak to you, he'll ring you". And he put the phone down.

I was shocked and crushed. What had I ever done, apart from love their son? The rejection was just awful. Now I look back and think: why didn't I run a mile? I should have, but I didn't. I put on my smiley face and just hung in there. I was determined not to be beaten by them.

Whenever they were horrible to me, which was often, I tried my hardest not to let them see me hurting. I would smile and turn away. I didn't want them to know I was suffering at all. But of course, the truth was that I'd drive home and burst into hysterical tears, feel that massive lack of self-worth and be consumed by loneliness. But rather than tackling it, I'd just put on my armour of a smile and hope it would carry me out of there with grace, even though it did hurt like mad. I didn't want to give his father the pleasure of knowing he'd upset me. I didn't want to give him that victory. I suppose it's that old truism of never wanting to show any kind of vulnerability to a bully. That has been a theme throughout my life.

I was 22 when Stewart and I got engaged, and 23 when we married. It didn't get any better.

Stewart's parents were awful in the lead up to the big day. They weren't interested or enthusiastic about the wedding at all. It was their worst nightmare. My family, Stewart and I took care of everything.

In the year of our wedding, I was hit by a huge blow. My dear Minnie died within 18 months of me losing my grandad. I was absolutely heartbroken, and it played havoc with my mental health. I felt very alone and vulnerable because my sounding boards, my rocks, were no longer there.

I had decided to get married to Stewart earlier than we'd planned so we could be married on my grandmother's birthday. It would be a Christmas wedding. I'd wanted to do it so that every year that day would be a double celebration—my anniversary and her birthday. But it was a terrible mistake.

I realised just how wrong I was about the relationship and our marriage only three days after the wedding. Stewart had been "allowed" by his parents to take a few days away from the horses so we could enjoy some time together at home (our honeymoon wasn't booked until late February, to fit around Stewart riding his racehorses). But then, on Boxing Day, his mother rang our house insisting that Stewart come down to the farm and help his father.

"If you don't come down here now," she said. "Your father will sell all the horses and you'll NOT inherit the farm".

That was how it was from then on. Stewart was tied to his parents and the farm; he believed he had no choice as he wanted the farm, he loved farming life and the horses. And for that reason, he would never stand up to them.

So rather than having regained control of my life through getting married and owning my own home, I found myself in another situation where I had no control. I'd gone from being controlled by my dad, to now being controlled by my father-in law. And on top of that I was expected to be the main breadwinner, working full-time to pay for our marital home. It was not the recipe for a happy and contented life.

It wasn't that Stewart didn't work. He did. He worked very hard, and long hours. He just never got paid for it. He would be up having delivered milk on their retail milk rounds at

3am every morning. Then he would exercise the horses and work on the farm. To subsidise his lack of wages he would take on extra jobs on neighbouring farms as well, but for the hours he worked he was earning a pittance.

My dear granny had left me sufficient money in her will to be able to put a large deposit down on a beautiful little new-built cottage in a nearby village. We were very fortunate that that allowed us to have a small mortgage, which eased the financial pressure I was under to earn.

About a month after we were married, I called my mum and was crying my eyes out. "Mum," I said. "It's just not how I wanted it to be. Any of it!"

I didn't want my marriage to feel like a constant competition with my in-laws over who could 'win' Stewart. Or to feel all the time that I wasn't wanted, that I was second best. Once again, I felt like I was giving my all, but it wasn't good enough. I knew I was never going to be enough for them. Inside I was incredibly sad. I couldn't work out what on earth I had done to deserve this. I thought: "All I've done is given your son a beautiful home. I have supported him in everything he has wanted to do and I've got a great job, yet you still think I am not a suitable wife?"

It broke me. That was truly one of my lowest moments. In the first year of my marriage (after the loss of my grandparents) I began having panic attacks so bad I couldn't go anywhere by myself. That said, I couldn't stay in the house by myself either. I felt simultaneously entirely controlled and yet completely out of control. And there was no way out.

It got so bad that I was struggling to go to work. I'd have panic attacks in the car. But once again my employer didn't know a thing. I never told anyone what I was going through. Except my husband and my mum. I was embarrassed.

It got to the point where I knew I had to get help. I booked an appointment at the doctor and my mum came with me. I explained all of my symptoms and my feelings, and yet the unsympathetic doctor diagnosed me not with anxiety, but with asthma.

That was when I knew I was on my own. If the doctor couldn't help me, I was going to have to try and help myself. I was so depressed. All I could see was darkness. Everything just went black. I remember saying to my mum: "I just wish I could have an injection and make all of these feelings go away".

I became agoraphobic and I ended up leaving my job in the pharmaceutical industry. That was a blow because it was a really good job—I was a business development manager—but I couldn't continue. The anxiety was poleaxing. I was put on betablockers and they didn't work. I ended up putting them down the loo! Nothing worked.

Because I didn't want to be left alone in the house, I started going down to the farm with Stewart; riding the racehorses with him and delivering the milk in the morning, even though it meant getting up so early. It was easier to be up before 3am than to stay in bed by myself. I was just a mess. I was never suicidal, but I couldn't see any light at the end of the tunnel. It was a terrible, difficult, dark time.

Slowly I pulled myself out of it. I forced myself to get outside, even though short walks or short car journeys were a huge challenge. I realised no-one was coming to save me. My mum tried to help, but nobody really understood. I didn't even understand it. What helped to turn my life around was a leaflet I picked up at the doctor about the Alexander Technique. I called the number and the most lovely warm lady answered the phone. She listened intently to me telling her how I felt, and I clearly remember asking her if she thought she could help someone like me. She invited me along to her studio, and after working with her over a period of eight weeks I started to feel more in touch with me again. She recommended and introduced me to a homeopath, and together they were a fundamental part of my healing journey.

It wasn't a quick fix. I still couldn't drive because of the anxiety. Stewart would take me to my treatments and patiently wait outside. I made little baby steps forward, tiny little steps of progress, and after a year or so I found I was able to drive and start creating some form of normality again.

We weren't going to be able to manage financially in the long term if I didn't return to work, so once again I pushed myself on through my fear and took another full-time job.

Chapter Four

William

I had only been in the new role for around six months when I found out I was pregnant. At 28 my son William was born. From the moment he arrived I understood what love was. I'd never felt that overwhelming feeling before, but I knew immediately that being a mother was the most special and important thing I've ever been gifted. It was my purpose.

That said, he weighed a mega 9lb 2 ounces! So he was always going to be my only child.

I was never offered the opportunity to stay at home and be a full-time mum, or even a part-time mum. It was just expected that I would go straight back to full-time employment.

I dreaded that day. I remember preparing to leave the house on my first day back to work after maternity leave. I was absolutely heartbroken at the thought of leaving my gorgeous baby for a full day, every day. Yet all Stewart could say was: "How am I supposed to cope on my own?" I pointed out that he didn't have to, as my mum was there to help.

This is where the pain became too much for me. I became resentful, and I couldn't forgive Stewart for not stepping up and offering me the opportunity of being a hands-on mum. I wanted to be at home with my gorgeous boy.

I hung on to our marriage for a lot longer than I should have, but in the end I made the decision I had been putting off and separated from Stewart when William was two. He went back to the farm to live with his mum and dad.

So they won. They got what they wanted. I sold our home and moved back in with my parents. Our marriage was over.

The breakdown of that relationship was a hard time. I was a new mum. I was the breadwinner working full-time. I was fighting to keep Stewart with me against his family's wishes and I got to a point where I just thought: "I can't fight for you anymore. I haven't got the energy. I can't fight for you, try to be a good mother to William, hold down a stressful full-time job, and run a home". And all of that was particularly impossible against a backdrop of constantly trying to prove I was good enough for his parents. The death knell of the marriage, though, what really killed it for me, was that Stewart would never fight for me. He would never stand up to his parents and say he loved me; that I was *his* choice, it was his life and they should just deal with it. Eventually, because he wouldn't go into battle for me, because he wouldn't put me first, I decided I was better off on my own, fending for myself with my son. So that's what I did.

It was really sad, of course. It wasn't that I didn't love Stewart. I did. But I wanted him to fight for me and he wouldn't. Even if he'd just said to his parents once: "you can keep your farm and even keep your horses. I'm going to go and get a job and I'm going to support my wife and my child". That would have just been so powerful for me. But he couldn't do it. He just didn't know how to. He was just too frightened of his parents. It wasn't even that he was desperate to inherit the land. More that he felt obliged to do it because it had been drilled into him from when he was such a small boy. It was like their family mantra: this is all for you, we are all doing this for you. This is your future. He was guilt-tripped into having to conform.

So there I was, divorced, living back with my parents and William, when I was offered the opportunity to join a local leisure and events company. Originally I was to be appointed as their Director of Sales, but then they offered me a share in their business and I became a Board Director. The company had a partnership agreement with a large hotel group to offer leisure activities at their resort-based hotels, and we'd offer lots of fun experiences: quad biking, clay pigeon shooting, off-road driving, and treasure hunts for families. The activities were a great success and corporates who were staying for conferences would often book them for team-building days.

Around a year after starting my new job, a sale board went up on a house right opposite where we were living with my parents. This was a rare opportunity not to be missed.

It would be a dream come true if I could afford it. It was the perfect house, just the right size, with three bedrooms, a lovely garden and an ideal location. It meant that I could go to work and William could just hop across the road to his granny and grandad's and they would be able to look after him until I returned home. We would have our own space. It was all looking so good.

I got in touch with my financial advisor and asked him if I could afford the asking price, and to my delight he said I would be able to get a mortgage. I went straight around to see the owners and offered them the asking price. I didn't want to lose the opportunity for my son and I to have our dream home.

They accepted my offer and within a few months we were getting our furniture out of storage and creating our home, a safe place for my son and I. We were both so excited.

The events business was going well and now we had our own home. I was back in a really good place, but there was one thing missing. I really wanted to have my own horse, and I had an urge to start competing again.

Stewart and I had stayed on good terms, and he was always an excellent father to William. His parents revelled in our separation; it was their badge of honour that they were right all along, that we would never work. They were right, it wouldn't, because *they* wouldn't allow it to.

William was a lot more interesting to Mamma Dot (as he fondly called his grandmother) once he was big enough to ride ponies. She delighted in the fact that she had another budding jockey coming through, so she went out and bought him a show pony and Stewart would lead him in competitions. It was a dream come true for her. Her son was back at home and at weekends she had her grandson fulfilling her dream.

I would go to the shows in my car to watch William ride, and it was here that I ignited my passion to compete again.

I started to ring around my old equestrian contacts looking for a show horse to buy. I had spotted one at a competition that I really admired. He was the most beautiful grey horse I had seen for a long time. I asked the owner if she would consider selling him, but at that time she declined my offer.

A few months had passed and I hadn't seen anything that I liked as much as that beautiful grey. I was so disappointed that the lady wouldn't sell him. I nearly gave up looking, but then when I was on a lunch break at work and just flicking through my address book, the name of a man I knew who had always had nice horses jumped out at me. I decided to give him a call. Well, I nearly fell off my chair. The beautiful grey horse was in his yard to be sold. How was that for fate playing its hand?

Without missing a beat, I arranged to go and see him that weekend. Stewart came with me to try the horse too, and within an hour of arriving to see him I had bought him.

He was called The Earl of March. Oh, what fun we had. He made my heart smile, not just my mouth. I competed him in hunter classes and side saddle. We won so many County Shows together, and we even qualified for The Royal International Horse Show and The Horse of the Year Show.

Joseph would be the pet name our son gave him, and this wonder horse rebuilt my confidence and self-belief. When I was riding him I felt as free as a bird. He was the horse of my dreams, and I had bought him myself with my hard-earned money.

Work was getting incredibly busy. In fact, it was going so well that the hotel chain we were working with offered us the opportunity to be a "preferred" supplier for all their 16 hotels, 11 more than we were contracted to do at that time. We would have a five-year contract. It seemed too good to be true!

There was only one hitch. We were a team based in the north-east of England and many of the hotels were in the Midlands and the south, so they said if we were to win the contract we needed a Midlands head office to make us more accessible for events. In order to deliver this request we would have to make a massive financial investment: new office space, warehousing, staff and equipment. After many meetings and much consideration, it was agreed by the board that we would push on and sign the contract, as the potential seemed huge. I have to say I was always trepidatious. I mean we weren't being given 'exclusive supplier' status; we were stumping up big money but there weren't any solid guarantees.

To raise the large amount of funds required for this huge project, we had to raise finance, and as a director I was expected to put my house forward as my personal guarantee against the loan. I didn't tell my father about it. I knew he would think I was crazy (and he would have been spot on).

Knowing what I do now I would never do that deal; all our eggs in one basket and no exclusivity? We must have been bananas. But for a while it looked like a good idea, and we brought in more business.

Chapter Five

Losing it all

What follows really was the darkest chapter in my life. My nadir. I'd had a bad feeling about putting my house up as collateral to fund the hotel contract and I certainly didn't share with my family that I had done it, which wasn't a good sign.

My house is my safe haven. I have a pretty stone characterful semi-detached cottage with three bedrooms and a lovely big garden backing onto open fields where cattle graze. An idyllic place for a child to grow up. I thought when I bought it that all my Christmases had come at once. I had a real sense of pride that I'd been able to do that, that I had a mortgage and could buy it in my own right, a real cosy home with a log burner where my son and I could just be.

William had a beautiful big bedroom, there was just so much space. I felt like I could breathe. Having left Stewart, it was absolutely perfect, particularly because it was just opposite mum and dad's house. The typical cottage with beautiful pink roses rambling up the front. I could see myself growing old there—it was my forever home. I just knew I would never want to move. It had everything and was in the area I wanted to be in, while my parents were right there on hand to help. It was perfect.

It's funny looking back now. I had such high-functioning anxiety then, and I was so worried about taking on all of the debt to build the business. My memories are just a blur, like my mind has deliberately wiped it out.

I know that the consensus on the board was that we were investing in the business to build it up and sell it one day. I too thought it was an opportunity; we were one of the biggest event leisure companies in the UK. I was in my mid-30s, it was exciting and from the outside it all looked perfect. I was driving a nice car, had designer clothes and luxury handbags, my best horse ever, and a lovely son. But inside, once again, it was a different story: the truth was I was living on my nerves.

I owned this fancy car, but I was still so anxious that I couldn't go on any long-distance drives on my own. I certainly couldn't drive solo on a motorway. The very idea filled me with dread. So to carry out business appointments I would always make an excuse to take a member of staff or someone with me. I was always OK if someone was with me, but on my own I was terrified. The panic attacks would get me so that I wouldn't be able to breathe; they had been so bad in the past that I was permanently scared I would have another one. I was paralysed with anxiety.

It was a terrible cycle. When I felt anxiety, it was mimicking the start of a panic attack, which was then bringing on a panic attack. I was living in a cycle of fear. I felt debilitated by it all. I didn't tell anyone, of course. I didn't go to the doctor either. I just swigged Rescue Remedy and got on with it! I hid it well, frightened of what people would think of me if they knew the truth.

I was never someone who would turn to alcohol. In fact I would never drink if I was under pressure, I'm the opposite of that. If ever I've got something to deal with, I have to do it in the cold light of day. I would never have a crutch like alcohol.

That's my steely side. It lives alongside my vulnerability, and they fight each other all the time. These days I can share those vulnerable feelings with my family, they know it is part of me, but back then I was so ashamed by the marriage break-up, my worries about the business deal and putting my house up as collateral that I didn't tell anyone. I'd already failed in my eyes and just felt not good enough, so I kept all the worry to myself and focused on being a good mum and spending as much time with my son as I could, in our happy place.

The new events contract was partially working, but we had invested a lot more money than we were getting out. We couldn't make the sums add up. And then the knockout punch came. The company we had the agreement with sold their hotel business.

That's when the rot set in. Within a few months, the majority of the managers, the general managers of the venues, and our non-executive director from the hotel side just disappeared. There was a complete change of management. The key people we worked with, the ones we had the relationships with, were gone, literally overnight. There was no-one left who understood the partnership.

We'd invested all this time, effort, and money in this contract, thinking that this was going to be the big one, and it all just seemed to fall away. On top of that it was 2008 and a big recession, which hit all of our big corporate clients hard. They were no longer in a position to spend money on luxury events.

Very soon, we had more money going out than we had coming in. We tried to put more money back into the business, but in hindsight that was a mistake. It was like pouring water into a sieve, and it was never going to be enough. It was such an incredibly bad and sad situation. In the end, we just had to make the torturous decision to close the business.

In August of 2008, I shut my office door for the last time.

All of the stress made me terribly anxious. Not surprising really. My life was spiralling out of control and I couldn't stop it. One of the side effects of this was that I no longer felt safe riding my beautiful horse. I found myself feeling scared whenever I sat on him, and if he moved suddenly, I was having panic attacks.

He was confused and I was confused. It wasn't long before I had to stop riding altogether. I was heartbroken. I had no idea why this was happening to me and I couldn't do anything about it. I didn't want to pass my lack of self-confidence on to him, so when the lady who coached me to ride side-saddle asked if she could have him on loan, I made the painful decision to let him go to her. Looking back, this is one of the biggest regrets of my life. I was not in a fit state mentally and should never have made that decision. He was my best friend. Sadly, he became ill with her and had to be put down. My heart breaks when I think of my beautiful Joseph.

Back in the business world, the news was equally grim. We owed more than we could pay back. As directors of the company we had given personal guarantees on the finance for the much-needed equipment. My house was on the line. With no job and no wages—and the debts I had—I couldn't pay my mortgage.

I had to declare myself bankrupt, and my home got handed over to the court.

I cannot describe the hole of worthlessness, of failure, of not being good enough, that I entered then. It was blackness. Every time I thought there might be a chink of light, I'd end up back there. It was like the universe was telling me: "Don't get above yourself. You're not good enough. You've got to remember you are not good enough. And if you forget, I'm gonna remind you".

I felt like my head was going to blow off. I couldn't breathe. I felt so out of control. The only thing I'd had to hang on to after the killer blow of the divorce was my financial independence. Financial stability had always been a rock to me, ever since I got my first job as a teenager. Now I had lost that, too. I felt trapped. That I had lost my freedom.

The reality of bankruptcy was grim. I'd never had any debt in my life, now I was a bankrupt with all the stigma that brings. I was still living in our home, but I knew that was temporary, and that William and I would have to leave.

I had no bank account. They took all my chequebooks, my debit and credit cards. I had no way of getting money. I had the worst possible credit rating. In fact, I couldn't get any credit of any kind for at least a year. I just hoped my income support would come through the post.

My parents were supportive. My situation was so bad that there was no judgement. My dad always strives for perfection, he has such high expectations of himself. So he puts himself under immense pressure, and that pressure had spread out to me too. But on this occasion, there was no "serves you right". It was just "how can we help"?

They looked after William when I needed space and they cooked for us most evenings. My mum came to the job centre in Consett with me so I could sign on. It was like another world. I sat down next to a young guy, who turned to me and asked: "What are you doing in here?"

I replied: "I've lost my job, I've lost my business, I'm about to lose my home, I've got nothing. How about you?"

He said: "I fell off the roof. I haven't got a job. I can't work. Do you wanna buy a knock-off mobile phone?"

I thought "Mum! What the hell is happening? How on earth has it come to this?"

Luckily, I got a great employment advisor, a really sympathetic gentleman. I chatted to him, explaining all that had happened and said: "You don't know me at all, but I don't want to get a job. I want to start my own business. I don't know what it's going to be at the moment, but will you please just give me a little time? Don't send me to job interviews, give me a couple of weeks to make sense of this whole situation. I am going to build a business, but I don't know what it is or how I'm going to do it. But I just know that's what I need to do".

There was a pause. Probably one of the most important pauses of my life.

He smiled at me. "We'll review it in 2 months," he said. "See what you're up to". And he signed me up for Income Support. I would get an Income Support book, the ones with the slips that tear off, that you take to the Post Office in exchange for cash. It wasn't what I was used to, but it was a lifeline.

I went home and I was in a mess mentally. I sat in the house on my own. I'd never not worked. I'd never not had money. William went to school, and he was on free school meals, which was something we'd never had to do before. The silence at home was deafening. There is only so much you can clean and iron to fill your days. I got so sick of watching morning TV, it was horrific.

My survival mechanism was to keep busy. I had the cleanest house, the best ironed clothes. I focused on being the best mum and cooking wholesome food; I've always been a home cook, I make comfort food; cottage pie, hot pots and cakes. You can make a lot of that on not much money. I just tried to do the best I could with what I had. But I realised pretty fast there is only so much ironing and watching Jeremy Kyle that anyone can take. I had to break this cycle before it sucked me in and broke me down completely.

Chapter Six

The turning point

Alongside the domestic chores, the sadness and the stress, there was huge amounts of administrative work; everything that goes with closing down a business. Also, because the 2008 recession was so bad, house prices had dropped and many homes were being repossessed and in negative equity. In a way the general chaos of the recession helped me. I'll explain how.

One day, around a month after I had been to the job centre, I looked out and there was a man in a suit standing in my garden. I opened the window and shouted out: "Who are you? What are you doing on my property?"

He came over, very politely, and said: "Oh I'm here from the bank. I need to value your house; I'll be taking photographs and measurements because it's about to go up for auction".

I wept then. It was really happening. I had to believe it.

It was a long afternoon. We started to chat as he took the pictures and got out his tape measure to work out how much my beloved home was worth.

I discovered that he'd also lost his job and he was doing part-time valuations to make ends meet. I made him a cup of tea and I asked him what he believed our home was worth. I told him what it had previously been valued at and what my mortgage was, and he said: "Your house is actually in negative equity now".

The house was worth less than my mortgage.

That sounds like a terrible thing to hear, but it gave me a bit of hope because I thought if my house is in negative equity there is no benefit to the bank to have it.

That made me think. At times like this it's like there is an inner voice, an inner compass (the one I try and help people find with my I CAN Method that is at the back of this book). Deep inside, that voice spoke to me.

"Sarah" the voice said, "you need to stop wound-licking and get off your backside. You've got to make something happen here. Because potentially you might be able to get your house back".

I will never know what possessed me to think I could ever do that from the parlous financial state I was in. I still don't know. But I just had this massive headline in my brain: "I can't let my son lose his home if there's any kind of chance I could keep it". And in that moment I could see a chink of light, a possible way through. And I embraced it.

I suppose the root of that determination, that force, was that I was trying to protect William. He was coming in from school saying our neighbours were revelling in our misfortunes, he told me: "Kids are saying we've gone belly-up mum, you've lost everything and we are poor". He'd come in from the school bus so upset, he was getting the brunt of that. Being bullied, like I was as a child. I hated that. His suffering was a huge spur to me to DO something. I just decided to fight with every fibre of my being, give it all I had.

It sounds weird but my starting point on the road to inspiration and recovery was getting another dog. Agoraphobia was sneaking up on me again and I thought if I had a dog I would have to walk it every day, that there would be constant motivation to get outside.

I always get my best ideas when I am walking; it helps stop the whirring thoughts and makes me concentrate on the big picture.

I found a litter of lurcher puppies advertised in the local free paper, looking for a good home. They were really cheap, too cheap to be honest. They'd been living in a shed on an allotment.

Stewart took William and I to see them. I'd have taken them all if I'd had the money. But I had to choose just one; I selected the runt of the litter, I empathised with him because he looked like he was getting bullied and pushed around. So we brought him home and we named him Sam. And from that day on he never left my side. He was my tireless ally and sounding board.

From the day Sam arrived I would walk, whatever the weather, with mum and him. Brainstorming, talking my mum's ears off. We chatted about all sorts of things, including my brother, who'd just got married before our business closed.

I'd sorted out the reception for him through my events company and I was moaning about the linen company. We'd wanted pretty chair covers to make the room look beautiful, but when they arrived the colour was all wrong and there weren't enough for all of the guests. But when I complained they wouldn't take any responsibility. They refused to be held accountable. I'd had such a battle to get my money back and it had been so disappointing. Very poor customer service.

I began fixating on that linen and the experience—how they must have let down so many other clients. How there was nothing to be done on the day if the linen turned up and it was disappointing.

I began to think about other events when I'd ordered chair covers for work. How often they didn't fit, and how the company who provided them didn't care, didn't stay around to fit them. And I suppose that was my eureka moment.

I thought "there's an opportunity here to create a fantastic service for luxury weddings and events. If a client can dream it in terms of event linen, then I can make it". We would offer a quality and reliable service with a product that would give their special day its own unique and memorable style.

I can remember saying to my mum: "We could do a fully fitted package!" The chair covers would be made to fit the chairs, we would fit them ourselves and we'd hand press them on the day to make sure that they weren't creased, ensuring that they were beautifully presented with care and attention. And we could offer stunning decor for these chairs, organza and satin bows, sure, but all sorts of other colours, fabrics and original designs.

My imagination was running riot.

As soon as I got home, I turned on my computer and started looking into who else was offering such a service. Where were they located? How much were they charging? I felt creative, a spark was ignited, something I hadn't felt for a very long time. I looked at leading fashion designers and their catwalks from the current seasons to find inspiration for colours and trends.

I was suddenly starting to feel alive; like a water lily which has been closed tight when it was dark, but was starting to open towards the light. That tiny chink eventually became a beam.

I rang my mum and enthusiastically told her: "I'm going to write a business plan; I really think this idea can work".

At the very least I knew it would give me something else to focus on.

In retrospect it seems crazy. I had no idea where to source that kind of linen, I had no factory, no contacts, I knew nothing about how to make them. But I had a dream. I started to look into it all.

During my research, I came across a company in America which supplied beautiful linen to the Oscars, the Met Ball and all these glamorous events. Opulent styles and designs I had never seen before. I found the telephone number of the CEO and rang her up, and to my delight she took my call. I told her my story, shared my idea and said there was no-one in the UK offering anything like the stunning designs she was supplying.

I asked if she might supply me. Unfortunately, I couldn't afford the proposal she offered at first, but if I did get my business going she very kindly agreed to sell me some of her "last year" designs to use as samples, at a heavily discounted price, as she never carried the designs forward. This was a very high-end business and I aspired to be like her.

I sat for weeks building a business model. One that would be strong and flexible and wouldn't contain any fixed overheads of the kind that had pulled down the events business. I knew what I didn't want. I didn't want a corporate office. I didn't want full-time employees. I didn't want to earn a huge amount of money. I wanted to make enough so I could pay my mortgage, to just have a nice little life with this business and make sure that I could be an available mum. To be at home for William going to school, be at home for him coming back from school, but have a business which would keep us afloat and allow us to afford doing the things we enjoy.

As I worked through the business model I realised that if I asked the clients to give me a 50% deposit upfront on booking our services, that would give me some cash flow. I'd make sure they paid me 21 days before their wedding or event so that I had the money in the bank. There would be no chasing debt.

Then I had my real brainwave. I believed that if I could get my service included in the hotels' wedding packages, I could learn exactly how many weddings the hotels were doing, how many guests were going to be there, and the date of their event. I could charge the hotels per chair for a fully fitted service, and I could suddenly work out my forecast of how much I could potentially earn each month. If I could only get these hotels on board, I knew I could solve their pain point of fitting the chair covers on the day of the wedding for them. I would come and do it all as part of the service. The hotels could hand their client to me and I would work on behalf of the venue, helping them design and style their wedding. I worked out that I needed at least five hotels to take on my service if I was to have a chance of saving our house and building a sustainable business.

That week (if ever there was a sign for me to not give up) I got a letter through the post from the bank saying that my mortgage rate had changed dramatically. I'd gone from being on a fixed rate of something like 7%, where my monthly mortgage was £1,200 a month, to being put onto a variable rate meaning my mortgage was to be reduced to £420 a month. This was potentially life-changing for me. I just knew I had to find a way to be able to pay it. There was no rent that could be any cheaper, so I had to make this business idea come to fruition.

But when it came to setting up the business, which was now looking like a goer, I was in a fix because I didn't have a bank account. Of course, you can't trade without one, but everywhere I tried I got the same response: "No way! You're a bankrupt single mum on income support. You may have a business plan but you know, let's be real here". Nobody would back me. It was back to the drawing board, and I was so frustrated.

I calculated that the least I needed was around £3000 to start the business. This would allow me to get some samples made and some sent over from America, and then I would have something to show to the local wedding venues in order to get their feedback.

At one point I did think I was going to have to give up on my dream, until I was flicking through my address books and saw the name Business Link, which was a government-run enterprise agency. We had done work for these people in my previous business, running team-building days for them. I dialled up the number, just hoping for some general advice. I was so fortunate that such a helpful man, Stan, answered the phone. I've never forgotten his name. That phone call and that gentleman changed my life.

Over the phone I shared my story with Stan and told him of my idea and business plan. To my delight, he invited me to meet him at their offices in Hexham, where I could present my plan to him in greater detail.

"So how are you, what happened? How have you ended up in this situation?", he asked. At this point I burst into tears. It was as if someone had released a pressure valve and I cried and cried. I was finally able to show my vulnerability to someone outside the family who I knew understood. He was amazing, he just kept feeding me tissues, and though he might have been thinking: "Dear Lord, how do I handle this?", he was a huge support.

Eventually, when I composed myself and I stopped crying, I was able to present him with the plan. He listened, he asked questions and then he said: "That's a really good idea. I think that could work. Leave it with me and we'll see what we can do".

Oh my word, I could have kissed him! I didn't, but believe me, I skipped out of that office with hope in my heart.

A few days later I got the best call. He rang me to say: "Yes! We can give you a start-up grant, even though you are bankrupt, so long as you set up as a sole trader, not as a limited company".

However, I still needed a bank account for the funds and to get my business started. Panic set in. Nobody would give me a bank account. What on earth could I do.

I turned to Google and typed in 'Bank accounts for bankrupts'. This amazing forum came up and highlighted the Co-Op Bank and its Cashminder account. They would give you a debit card, but no overdraft or credit card. But that didn't matter. It meant I could pay money in, draw money out, buy things over the phone and do online banking. I applied for an account, and to my absolute relief I was accepted. The day I got one was like a miracle. I felt like I was starting to get my life back. My shackles were being removed.

There I was. I had a small business grant, a fantastic business plan, a bank account, and the possibility of saving my home. All I had to do now was sell chair covers and come up with a name for the business.

One Saturday afternoon I was sat with my family, coming up with all sorts of ideas for what to call the company, when I pitched up with, "Let's keep it simple, we'll call it Simply Bows and Chair Covers, it will do what is says on the tin". That was it. Simply Bows and Chair Covers was born.

I had all the suppliers for the accessories, but I didn't have anyone to make chair covers and I certainly couldn't sew. My dad remembered a lady in a local town who manufactured flags, and he figured that if she could make flags, she would have a sewing machine, understand about fabrics and (if nothing else) may be able to offer some sound advice. I got in touch with her and she offered more than advice, she said she knew how to make chair covers and would be delighted to work with me and help me to get my business started.

The pressure was now intense. I had no idea how long I had left in my house, and I was waiting for the letter to drop through the door at any time. Remember that I am an anxious person, and my self-belief then could NOT have been any lower. It was at rock bottom, lower than a snake's belly on the grass, as my Minnie would have said.

I had a head full of design ideas and needed to get them manufactured into product. I was anxious, but equally so excited to see my designs brought to life. I arranged with my suppliers to get some samples made, which I paid for from the business grant that I had received, and I sold all of my 18th and 21st birthday jewellery that my grandparents had bought for me—I knew that if they were there they would agree to it. "This is it, my little idea is being brought to life", I thought to myself. I was now ready to present to potential customers.

This was such a hard task for me. I had such a mix of emotions. I was full of hope, but my imposter syndrome was having a field day. I would be judged, I would be mocked, who would believe in my idea? No, I can't do it. Then I looked at the alternative: my son can lose his home, or I can put my purpose ahead of my fear and pull my finger out, push through those self-limiting beliefs.

I started by calling clients I had worked with in my previous business. I thought it easier to contact warm leads who I had a connection with. I decided from the beginning to share with them the full story of how and why I was starting this business, and that I was bankrupt and starting from scratch. I had learnt a harsh lesson: contracts don't secure business, relationships do. Business is sound when it is built on people you know, like and trust.

The response to my business model and my products from our initial telephone calls was so positive that many of the wedding managers I spoke to invited me into their venues to present to them what I had to offer. What a huge relief to hear some positivity; there was a glimmer of light at the end of the tunnel.

Now I needed to get out into the big wide world again. I had to face my fears, and also the fact I didn't have any transport! Weirdly, my old company car, a snazzy Range Rover, was still sat on the drive; the contract hire company hadn't collected it even though I regularly chased them. So I made a plan. I would insure the company car for a day at a time when I had an appointment, and I would take my mum with me for moral support!

She was like a hostage. I was carrying the pain of failure and this was really amplifying my anxiety. I didn't want to do anything on my own, let alone pitch for new business. Mum was such a rock to me. She came with me to all my meetings with the hotels. The worst part was reiterating to the hotels what had happened to me. That I was bankrupt. I didn't want potential clients hearing my story from a third party, where it had the chance to be manipulated. I had a policy of total honesty because I thought that would be the best thing for the relationship moving forward.

I wanted to build a relationship where my clients felt I added value to them, so they would see the benefit I would bring to them. I wanted them to want to work with me, not for me to push the sale.

My warehouse was a small silver suitcase, and I literally pulled my whole business around in this little box on wheels. It housed all my stock, which consisted of a small but beautiful selection of samples and fabrics which I proudly pulled out to present to my prospective clients, holding my breath with nervous anticipation over how they would receive them.

To my delight, the hotels I really wanted to work with loved my fresh approach and the edge my designs had over previous suppliers they had used. They loved my ideas and soon offered me the opportunity to become their preferred supplier. They genuinely loved what I did and understood how it would enhance their wedding offerings. It wasn't long before I was taking bookings and raising invoices. To see some money going into my bank account was such a confidence boost. I was so proud.

It was a wonderful feeling going back to the job centre to see the gentleman who offered me time and trusted me. To tell him I was true to my word and had created the business I dreamed of. I was signed off from income support!

The first event we confirmed was at the Durham Marriott, Royal County Hotel, for 30 white chair covers for a young lady's 21st birthday party, and they would each be decorated with gorgeous, fluffy baby pink organza bows. I remember it as if it were yesterday.

Mum and I were nervous and excited in equal measure to be styling our first-ever event. We arrived in the room and looked at each other for reassurance before slowly dressing one chair at a time. The first few bows were hard to tie as we were so anxious, but we soon got the hang of it. We'd been practicing tying bows on our kitchen chairs for weeks prior to the event. Even dad had been practicing with us; in fact my dad came up with a genius idea to put two colours together and then split them open like a butterfly, which became our signature design in the early days.

The interest in Simply Bows and Chair Covers started to gather pace and very quickly we were making regular monthly sales. At this point it seemed there was a real possibility that I might be able to reclaim our home.

Mum and Dad were very keen for me to try. I negotiated with the bank to see if we could come to an agreement. We figured if the house was in negative equity, they might be keen to talk to me if I could start paying my mortgage back and repay the arrears.

It was then that I reluctantly took dad up on his offer of a short-term loan. I'd never borrowed money from my family, but this gesture was so welcomed, and I made the call to the bank.

Well, I gave it the sales pitch of my life and I was blown away when they told me that they would accept my request. We had to pay the bank £1 for the title deeds to release them from the bankruptcy, and then I was to pay the arrears (thank you dad!). The day I knew I wasn't going to lose my house was one of the sweetest of my whole life.

It took about seven months from when I first set up the business to that day, when I knew I would be in a comfortable position to start paying my mortgage. I felt like I was starting to come alive again. My life was rebuilding, and this time on my own terms.

Chapter Seven

Success

The next chapter of my life was much happier. In that first year of Simply Bows and Chair Covers I made a multiple five-figure profit. The business consisted of me and my mum, and we did everything ourselves, so obviously there were no external costs. We were often delivering and styling up to 15 weddings a week, and it became insane. Many of the luxury hotels in the North East of England had my service as part of the wedding package. I was driving all over the place!

Then the business took off to the point where we very nearly couldn't manage it with just the two of us anymore. I brought in my first member of staff, a local lady who would work for me part-time, fitting chair covers. I was very careful with money, ensuring we ran on minimal expenditure and reinvested any profit back into the business. That allowed me to buy a little van; our first company vehicle. My little idea was establishing itself as a small business.

We were growing rapidly, so much so that I was having to turn down bookings that were duplicated on the same day, certainly not something I wanted to do, but I was in a bind. I didn't want to bring other people into the firm and then have to start renting premises. I felt safe with it just being us and having very manageable overheads. I was afraid of history repeating itself and getting my fingers burned again.

I was very much about quality, service and design; that was what my name stood for. I felt very proud of the company.

It was all mine. But I knew realistically that I needed to expand. I kept going round and round in my head on this conundrum. I could see so much opportunity, but fear of failure was holding me back. What if it all went wrong? Playing small seemed safe.

It was my dad who suggested a franchise model. The more I looked into it, the more I liked the idea. I had worked in franchising before and could see the opportunity. Franchising allowed me to expand, but also to keep control; to create my own model for others to follow. Franchisees would invest in the business financially; I would have their "buy in" and in my eyes this meant they would commit to getting a return on their investment. They would work hard and be accountable for their success. They would want it to work and be more committed than an employee, and more importantly they would pay me to allow them to trade under my licence.

That was how I did it: I sat down and wrote an operations manual which was like a bible for how an event should be organised and how the business was to be managed.

Franchising the brand would allow me to have national offices without the fixed overheads.

I decided to test the water locally. As the North East office was at full capacity, I could see the opportunity of splitting it into counties.

I appointed a top Franchise Solicitor to write our business contract and terms, trademarked the name, collated a package and looked to appoint my first franchisee.

Before I even had the opportunity to advertise for a franchisee, I was approached by a super lady who had worked in weddings and events and was looking for a job. I suggested she might like to join me as a franchisee and run her own business, but with my support and proven business model there to guide her.

Franchising worked for our business. Fast forward to now and I've got 10 offices, award-winners in their own right, with franchisees stretching from Dundee right the way down to South Wales and across the country.

It has been very important to me to get the right people, to ensure they share my ethos of delivering quality on every level. Even if they just style 20 weddings a year in, say, Cheshire, so long as they are beautiful weddings, that is 20 more than I would have done if I had played small. I didn't want to make a quick buck out of the wedding business. Compromising quality over growth was never my intention. I wanted to build a business that would stand the test of time, and that is exactly what we have created.

Becoming one of my franchisees makes becoming an entrepreneur very easy. That first tough step onto the rung of the success ladder is all taken care of. They are immediately part of a multi award-winning brand, with a proven business model, one that has been in every national newspaper on the back of its success. It's got credibility, a beautiful website with an extensive gallery, and testimonials coming out of its ears. It's a safe bet and I am there every step of the way to mentor them, to help get their business started, and to answer any questions they may have.

Simply Bows and Chair Covers became so successful that I started being recognised as an inspirational entrepreneur, and I was nominated for some high-profile business awards.

I won the business growth award for the Entrepreneurs' Forum, who support North East Businesses, in 2012. And then, as a member of the North East Chamber of Commerce, I won their Small Business Award—an entry into a bigger regional award, which I also won—and that put me into a

National Award. I was invited down to a glittering awards ceremony at the Guildhall in London, where I won the big award from entries right across the whole of the United Kingdom. They named Simply Bows and Chair Covers the most promising business in the UK in 2012.

With the award wins came a huge amount of national PR in some high-profile newspapers. I was on the front page of the Sunday Times business section, The Daily Mail, and Femail, and appeared in several glossy magazines. I did radio interviews too, and as more people heard of my success, more people wanted to buy franchises.

So I was winning all these awards, and it was all looking so good. I should have been over the moon.

But life is always more complicated than that. And it was around this time that Stewart's dad, my ex-father-in-law, was dying of cancer. Now you might say, "why was that an issue?" After all, we were divorced...

But as I said, life is complicated! Although we were separated, Stewart was always in my life; he was William's father and was always a real support to me. In fact, alongside my mum, dad and brother, Stewart was my rock. We're a very strong, close-knit family and even when we weren't together, Stewart was a part of that. In fact, when I was building up the business, we were so busy that Stewart had started helping out with the weddings, and when he had some money he gave it to me to get the franchise business off the ground!

I know, there is an irony in my ex doing that to be sure! But we always stayed friends, my door was always open. In fact, the night I was declared bankrupt Stewart and our best friend took me out for dinner. They always believed in me. They actually said even then: "You know you'll be alright, you'll be okay". That was a balm for me. They believed in me when I didn't believe in myself.

Stewart didn't have a lot of money to help me financially when things were tough, because his money was in his family farm. That was how it had always been. But he always helped me the best he could with William. And in 2010 it was his turn to suffer a tough time. His dad was dying of cancer, so I supported him as much as I could. Even though I had never had a good relationship with his father, I wanted to help Stewart, so I started to go back down to the farm to support him.

It's strange to think that I did that; it was the animosity between me and Stewart's parents and his inability to fight for me which led to the end of our marriage. But somehow when they started getting ill it was all different. His father was weak and I suppose I was stronger. I felt more confident and my priorities were different; my business was growing. And Stewart was losing his dad, I really felt for him; he was buckling and needed my support. On top of that the farm was not performing as well as it could have been, not innovating or going the way Stewart wanted it to go because his father was dying and all of his energy and attention was having to be focused elsewhere.

And then in 2011 his father died. It left Stewart to pick up the pieces and take on the role and responsibility he had always wanted, but not under those circumstances. It was incredibly tough, and he had a lot to sort out.

Shortly after that his mum also became very ill. And if that wasn't enough to be coping with, my own health took a downturn. I had suffered from fibroids for a while and then on top of that I developed an 8cm ovarian cyst. It was so bad that they decided the only fix was to put me into a chemical menopause at 40, with the drug Zoladex.

Now some of you readers are probably thinking: "isn't that too much information?" But I think it is important to be honest about the kinds of trials and tribulations female entrepreneurs face. And if you are a woman at this stage in life, I'm hoping my honesty about the physical aspect of my life and journey will help!

So there I was, running my business and getting all this acclaim, even fame. But privately I was in agony because of my health, because my heart ached for Stewart and his troubles, and because I was juggling it all while still being a good mum to our son.

They gave me the injections to try and shrink the fibroids, and then I had to have an operation, the equivalent of a hysterectomy, which any woman will know is a huge shock to the system.

I suppose I am writing this because the success I had with my business was bittersweet. Even after that terrible time I had been through and even though I was coming out the other side, it just wasn't easy for me to enjoy it, or really believe that the good times were rolling.

For instance, I was so ill when I won that big award at the Guildhall that I couldn't enjoy it at all. I was so anaemic; I could hardly stand up. There's a picture of me as the winner, and my hair is so thin, I literally look like it's all fallen out. I am pale, washed out. I just wanted to disappear.

And it wasn't just that I felt physically weak and ill, and emotionally worried about Stewart and his family. My mental health wasn't great either.

I'm afraid that winning those prizes didn't erase my imposter syndrome; if anything it made it worse. It triggered all my deep feelings of being unworthy, of not having the right to be there. There I was in this huge grand room rammed with 500 people all cheering my success, but I couldn't feel proud or positive; my anxiety was off the charts.

It's such a shame, I know, but despite the success, it was not a happy time. We'd gone through the death of Stewart's dad, and then almost immediately his mum was dying too.

I was so distracted and anxious about how Stewart was coping, and feeling so ill myself, that even sitting in that grand room waiting for the announcement of the prize I was sure I wasn't going to win. I wasn't even concentrating. When they called my name at the Guildhall I wasn't even listening. Stewart had to nudge me to go and collect the prize.

I suppose it is not surprising that I didn't make the most of it, or go and celebrate my success with the others.

That night, the Chamber of Commerce team asked me if I'd like to go to a swanky club in Mayfair to celebrate the win. I said no.

I didn't want to drink or cheer. I just went straight to my bedroom where I collapsed from feeling so weak, I was drained.

A few weeks after the award The Chamber asked if I would speak at their main conference, share with their delegates how I'd built Simply Bows and Chair Covers and my inspirational story. But I couldn't do it. Standing in front of 500 people filled me with dread. I turned down that wonderful opportunity.

Looking back now I have sympathy for my younger self. I understand what happened. I was just too scared. My self-limiting beliefs and my anxiety just went into overdrive. In my deepest self I just didn't think I could speak at that conference. I didn't have the confidence, I was still dealing with the shame of being bankrupt, the fear of being judged, and the imposter syndrome of feeling I didn't deserve to be asked.

How did I get out of it? I made an excuse and said that I was unable to attend because I had other commitments, or some other baloney. I felt so sad. There was a part of me that desperately wanted to do it, to celebrate the journey I had come on, and how much I had achieved. But the larger part of me just didn't feel capable of standing up there with all those eyes staring at me and sharing my story. So I turned it down. It was just too big an ask of myself at that time.

Now I regret that hugely. When I look back, I feel really sad for my younger self because it was a massive moment. I'd done so well but I just couldn't feel it. For me, starting the business was a means to an end. To save my house. To create a life for William. It wasn't about awards or glory. Just saving our skins.

Now, you're probably wondering what Stewart was doing with me at that Awards Ceremony. Well the truth is, we'd got back together, sometime in the maelstrom of his father dying and me trying to save the house—it's all such a blur. I was just in overdrive trying to muddle through. I'm not being coy, I just don't really remember the sequence of events. But after Stewart's mum died, we got remarried.

I know that sounds mad, but it's just how life was back then. Just muddling through, trying to keep everything together. Working together to survive.

Chapter Eight

A new life for the farm

Of course, life isn't just about business. There were many developments in my private life which I was juggling simultaneously with managing my fledgling company and the success it garnered. These are relevant because the next chapter in my life involved a huge property project with Stewart, the man I was married to, then divorced and then remarried.

Even though we had divorced, Stewart never really left my life; he was William's father and was always around and went on to be a real support to me. Furthermore, it was important to me that even though Stewart and I were divorced, this wouldn't impact on the relationship with his son.

Stewart didn't have the money to help me financially because his money was in his family farm. That was how it had always been. But he always helped me the best he could with William.

In 2010 it was his turn to suffer a tough time. I've already touched on how his mum and dad both died within 18 months of each other.

Because I still cared for Stewart, I wanted to support him in any way I could. I started to go back down to the farm, helping him with the milk rounds, both delivering milk and helping collect the milk money from his customers on a weekly basis.

There wasn't a big romantic moment when we got back together. It was a very organic kind of process. We spent more time together, one night he just stayed over, then that became a pattern and he never left!

But while my life was on an upward trajectory, for Stewart it was a different story. After his parents died he felt absolutely lost. His whole life had been lived appeasing his controlling mum and dad—he was their only son, and they literally ran everything for him. Granted this wasn't always great, but with them both gone the rug had been pulled from under his feet emotionally. He now had to get into the driving seat, and he found it daunting.

There were practical problems too. Whilst Stewart was caring for his parents he had brought in some outside help to keep the farm ticking over. They were doing the bare minimum and things had slipped quite dramatically. Cows were dying whilst calving, excuses were made, the milk round was tiring and not returning on the investment of the time it took up. Things were tough, and it was a hell of a period for him. He had 24 horses on DIY livery which were causing more problems. Things had to change.

We had to make some uncomfortable decisions. Stewart was living with me and William, which meant the farm was empty during the night. It is about 20 minutes away from our home, so that was not ideal for security. Stewart had decided that he didn't want to move back there because it held too many painful memories, particularly of tough times with his parents when they were ill.

It was a beautiful, small but tired farm set in the Tyne Valley in Northumberland, consisting of a farm cottage and a collection of traditional stone buildings that would have historically made up a granary, cart shed and buildings to hold the cattle. In later years Stewart and his family used it as stabling for their horses. One day when we were down there walking around the yard considering our options, I took his arm and said, "Look!"

The sun was shining on the stone buildings, reflecting like gold on the old sandstone. it was so beautiful, it just glowed, it looked alive.

"Why don't we try and get planning permission and see if we could breathe some life back into this place?" I asked. "Rather than selling it, or farming it, why don't we DEVELOP it?"

Stewart wasn't keen. He said his parents had tried to get planning permission to turn some of the outbuildings into properties, but they could never get it.

I gave him an eye roll. "Well why don't we put in for planning ourselves and just see," I said.

We appointed some professional help to support us with the planning consent. It took about 18 months to-ing and fro-ing with plans and design ideas, but I had found a brilliant planning officer to work for us, and he certainly earned his wages. Eventually we had our permission granted to build five beautiful barn conversions, some with three bedrooms, some five.

The next stage was to get some costs from builders to deliver our ambitious project. Then we had to determine how we were going to afford to do it!

Once again we sat down at my dining room table and set about making a plan. We decided that we could dramatically reduce the development costs if we took all the modern buildings down ourselves and stripped the site back ready for the builders to start work. Over the next

12 months Stewart, my dad and I were driving diggers, stripping back all the buildings to the original stone, removing the roofs. You name it, we did it. We prepared the whole site ready for the builder to just come in and start. I was out in all weathers in my work boots and my green boiler suit. I've got my HGV licence; I can drive a wagon, so a little Bob Cat was a breeze. It just shows what you can do if you really put your mind to it, have vision, are supported by a well thought out strategic plan and have a good team working with you.

We raised funds for the build by selling off parts of the farm in small lots.

First, I sold the farmhouse with three acres of land. Next, we sold a temporary cottage/mobile home with 15 acres of land. Then we sold another 90 acres of farmland separately. That raised enough finance to get the site prepared, services in and a couple of the houses finished and ready to sell, with the foundations laid and ready for the next three. Put like that it sounds simple, but of course the logistics of building and delays meant it didn't work out like that!

The pressure was on, because once we'd finished the first two barn conversions, we had to make sure we sold them quickly so we could continue with the build. It was very much build, sell, build, sell. At one point we nearly ran out of money and had to take a bridging loan for added comfort. That was very scary and something I really didn't want to do, because of my history and never wanting to have debt.

I had to keep reminding myself that it would be okay because we had more assets than debt. That there was no way we could lose everything.

But it just shows that we can overcome our fears and our self-limiting beliefs. Three years later we had completed the project and built five beautiful quality homes, fitted to the highest standard. We were very proud. We were able to pay back our loan and realise a healthy profit for our effort.

Chapter Nine

My melanoma and how my vanity saved me

In the midst of all the labouring on our building site, I decided to take some time out and have a self-indulgent day with my mum. We went to see an aesthetic doctor who had a wonder machine that could tighten and brighten your tired and saggy skin. Believe me, with the stress of the last few years my face needed all the help it could get! My mother had found the guy, and she decided I should get out of my scruffy boiler suit and come with her to suss him out. To be honest, we're both quite vain, have no intention of growing old before we need too, and we're both quite happy to do the work. So off we trotted in a state of great excitement at the prospect of turning back time!

So imagine this, I'm sitting in the specialist's chair, relishing not being at the wheel of a truck, or wielding a hammer, when he starts examining my face. He looks at a mole on the side of my head and then takes a magnifying lens. He peers at me again and then stands back with a serious expression on his face.

"Sarah," he said. "That mole on the side of your cheek, near your hair line. How long have you had it?"

I was really dismissive. "I don't know," I said. "A year? Six months?"

The mole was about the size of a five-pence piece, maybe a little smaller. It was brown.

"Has it ever itched?" he asked.

"Yes," I said.

"Has it ever bled?"

The answer was yes to that too.

There was a long pause. "I don't like the look of it," he said quietly.

I was still feeling cocky. "Well, why don't you like it? And what do you know about moles?"

It turned out that he wasn't just an aesthetics specialist.

"Well, in my other life I'm a skin cancer specialist".

At that point my blood ran cold.

"Sarah," he said. "I want you to make an appointment right now to get that mole taken off".

So I stepped out into the car park and made an appointment there and then to see a specialist.

The first thing I explained to him when we met was how terrified I was of hospitals.

"If I don't have to have this mole taken off, please don't make me," I said.

He could see I was very anxious. In a kind voice, he said: "If that's how you feel, why don't you wait another six months and then come back and see me and we will take it from there?"

I got up to leave the room. In fact, I got all the way to the door and put my hand on the handle to leave. But whoever my guardian angel is (I know I have one because it is the angel who changed my mortgage rate, who put the house valuer in the garden when my home was in negative equity and all of the other lucky things that have happened over the years), that angel said to me in a stern voice: "Sarah you are not going to walk through that door girl! You go back and sit down right now and agree to have that mole taken off".

So I did.

I walked back over to the doctor and said I'd changed my mind and he needed to take it off as soon as possible!

"Just do it," I said.

Once I'd decided to do it, I didn't think anything of it. I'd had two other moles removed when I was younger out of pure vanity. I did not consider there could be a problem.

A week later I was driving home from a day out with friends when my phone rang in the car. It was my specialist. He asked if I could pull over as he had some concerning news. He told me that my mole was a cancerous malignant melanoma and that I must have a second operation as soon as possible.

Oh my word, I was not expecting this news. A short drive home suddenly seemed very long. All I could think about was "what if I died?" Who would be there for my son? My son needs his mum, I need my son. I want to be there to see him grow up. Who will he turn to when he has a problem? I was so scared. So very scared. Not for me, but for my son, who could lose his mother.

I remember getting home and calling my mum and dad, who came straight over, and Stewart being there and telling them all the news. They were all very shocked.

The surgeon said it was very lucky that I'd had the melanoma taken off, as it would have continued to grow and could have eventually spread to my lymph glands. Then the cancer would have taken over and spread to other parts of my body. I probably would never have known, and it could have possibly been too late if left too long undiagnosed.

The next procedure was to have a belt-and-braces operation. A second procedure to remove all trace of the cancerous cells. He wanted to go back in and make sure there was a bigger margin around where the melanoma had been found, just to make sure they had got any dangerous tissue away. I had 13 stitches in my face. But my surgeon is brilliant, and you would never know it had been there.

It is strange when you have a health scare like that. I am sure people all have different ways of dealing with it. My way of coping was to try not to dwell on it. Work, as always, was my coping mechanism. I just wanted to get back to doing the weddings; I returned two days post-operation with stitches in my face. One bride came up to me while I was tying bows on chairs for her big day and asked: "What happened to your face?"

"Oh, I had skin cancer" I said, and kept tying the bows. She looked quite shocked. It definitely wasn't the answer she was expecting.

I don't think I am particularly stoic. My ability to just carry on, to smile through it, to hide my real feelings, goes back to that childhood bullying. I learnt then to put a grin on my face and just keep going. To say to myself: "It'll be fine" or "Of course you're scared but keep going". I know that doesn't work in the long term, but it is still my default coping mechanism.

The development was now complete and excited families were moving in. It had been one hell of a tough project for us all, both financially and mentally. Some parts were really draining. But in the end, we made the best of Stewart's birthright and we are incredibly proud that we pushed through. We did a good job!

And then, just as we sold the last house and we were tidying up the site, my eye was caught by the large modern cattle shed that we had been using for storage. It was to be taken down because we felt it was an eyesore and had no use for it. Walking through the yard with my dad and Stewart, a thought just popped into my head: I said, "Why don't we try and get planning permission for this shed?"

They groaned. Stewart shook his head, saying we'd never get any more planning permissions. "Look, if I can get planning permission and develop it into houses, can I have the money?" I joked. But I actually wasn't joking. I decided to approach my planning consultant to get his opinion on the potential of the project.

He came back to me with a positive response and again we set about applying for our second phase development—three single-storey homes with large gardens front and back and far-reaching views across the meadows.

The materials we were allowed to use on this project were very specific, and it had to reflect the design of the existing buildings. Once again there was a lot of to-ing and fro-ing and debating with the council, but we eventually got our planning permission.

Just as the planning was granted, I was diagnosed with skin cancer again. This time the malignant melanoma was on my chest. They picked it up on one of my regular six-month screenings. It was at a very early stage. Fortunately they got it off pretty quickly, and a second operation would give me the all-clear.

But it was worrying that they kept reappearing.

I just tried not to dwell on it. Got on with building my houses, delivering my weddings, managing my franchised business and, most importantly, caring for my son.

It had an effect though. It sounds strange but the true legacy of the cancer is this huge gratitude to still be alive. I am so grateful just to be here. It has totally transformed my way of thinking. Rather than being in an "Oh woe is me" mindset, these days I am just so thankful to be here; for the opportunity to live. The sky is bluer than it ever was before. The flowers are brighter and prettier and smell more fragrant. Colours are more vivid. When I walk my dog, I just feel full of a sense of joy.

In a funny way, it was after the cancer that I started to feel that I was really living, rather than just existing. It sounds crazy that you're diagnosed with cancer and it actually gives you life, but that is what happened. I felt like I had a rebirth, and I took too much for granted before. Now it is as if the world is in full technicolour. I feel fired up with purpose.

Chapter Ten

What do I do now? Project Sarah — how I turned my focus on ME

Part of this huge new happiness to be alive was an appreciation for the people in my life. But the converse was that it also focused me on everything I no longer wanted. It also made me think about being 49. For the first time, I realised that my time here is finite. It was a moment of re-evaluation. That sense that life is short.

I became more confident, and I decided to finally sort myself out and start living. I decided it was time to ditch the anxiety and panic attacks and live a fulfilled life.

Can you just decide to ditch those kinds of things from your life? Entrenched patterns that have dogged you since childhood? Well, yes. I discovered that you really can. But it takes work and commitment, just like setting up and building a business.

This period of time wasn't without its stresses. We eventually got all of the houses sold from phase one of the build, although we did have to rent one out for a short while as, frustratingly, the sale fell through at the last minute THREE times. With the support of another small bridging loan, the last house was sold and the site complete. At one point we had 24 hours to sell a house before the loan was due to be paid back. It was pretty high pressure. But it all worked out.

Including the cottages we sold ten houses, and all just before the pandemic hit—talk about lucky timing!

But even before lockdown I had acknowledged that I needed a proper break. Reading this, I'm sure you can understand that I was drained. I had already taken a step back from delivering weddings to focus on managing the franchise business.

The farm development was a financial success even though it was a huge challenge, pushing us far out of our comfort zone at times.

We still live exactly where we always did, in my lovely house. I have no desire to move. We've created a stable yard and equestrian facility for William. He is a talented horseman who has chosen producing young competition horses and coaching other riders as his profession. How funny to think that he has not only followed my dream, but is now living it. I couldn't be happier for him. When I am not working, I act as his groom when he competes at shows and events around the UK. We have a huge van which we live in; you can find me at all the big shows, taking Zoom meetings between mucking out and helping William in and out of the showing ring.

Could I stop working? Probably, but I wouldn't want to. It is wonderful to have more financial freedom than I have had before and not to feel owned by anyone. The best thing is that we can all do exactly what we want to do. The comfort of time and choice is a huge luxury. We've got a nice little life, and to me that is more important than focusing on getting extremely rich and miserable and having no proper time to enjoy all my effort.

But of course, the most important thing to have in life is purpose. It is when you don't have a purpose that your mind makes tricks, and your mental health suffers.

So there I was, my boxes all nicely ticked, job done. And then the pandemic hit.

And it could NOT have been worse. There was nothing for me to do and nowhere for me to be. I came to sharply realise that busy-ness had been a huge crutch for me; a distraction from my deep-rooted feelings, my reality.

I now had nowhere to run.

Busyness is an escape; busy was my addiction. It was like, keep busy, and everything will be alright. Because you're so busy you don't have time to think about anything else, to dwell, so just keep busy, keep avoiding.

But then busy stopped.

I started to feel anxious, I had too much time on my hands.

There was only so much baking and cleaning I could do.

I started to dwell on my failures like the bankruptcy. The fact that my wedding business was put on hold throughout the pandemic brought back harsh memories that I thought I had buried. I was worried that history was repeating itself, and I started to worry so much about money and our future.

I knew from past experience that I had to get outside and walk, like I had when I was contemplating ideas for my business. Sam was getting old and wasn't in good health, so he could only join me on short strolls, but it was always a comfort to have him by my side.

Eventually I ended up back at my faithful dining room table to make a strategic plan. But this time the plan wasn't for the business, or to save the farm, or to keep myself alive. It was Action Plan Me. There I was, a few months from 50, ready for a new chapter. But what could it look like? What could it be?

I felt like I was losing my purpose. I felt like I was becoming invisible. I was hitting 50 and I was thinking, "I don't like this. I've come through so much but now what? My son is grown up and knows exactly what he wants from his life. My husband is happy. But me: I need a purpose in my life, a challenge, a plan".

So I was like: what the hell am I going to do? I would sit on LinkedIn daily, reading posts from anxious business owners who were panicking and fearful and trying to diversify or pivot in order to survive the impact of the pandemic on their businesses.

I supported my franchisees on endless Zooms. I came up with a strategy for Simply Bows and Chair Covers so we could keep visible. We gave hundreds of tablecloths, hundreds of metres of fabric to the NHS so they could be made into scrubs. That was the least we could do. We ran competitions for couples whose weddings were postponed, gifting beautiful comfort hampers, and we held our clients' hands, nurturing them through the turbulent time. It kept my team busy and focused.

But apart from that, I felt stuck.

I decided to do a feasibility study on myself, in the same way I had done with all of my business projects before. Back to the dining room table I went. And I followed the proven system that I had put into action to build my business, to build my houses.

So there I am. It's the pandemic and I'm sitting at the dining room table, I'm writing, and I'm drawing, and I'm mind-mapping and networking. And I am asking myself big questions: "What do I want? Who am I? When did I last feel happy? What does happy feel like? What is my purpose in life?"

And what came out of that was:

1. I really wanted to pay forward the lessons I have learned through adversity.

2. I love mentoring and supporting people. I love to help people succeed, be the best version of themselves.

So there it was. I decided to become a Mindset and Business Mentor.

I am going to give something back.

And working out the strategy that I'd used to sort myself out, I realised there were lots of others out there who were probably also feeling stuck, at a crossroads, and who could also benefit.

So I put a stake in the ground and decided to put this way of thinking, my method devised while I sat at the dining room table, into a coaching programme.

I didn't have any experience of writing coaching programmes, but I had the methodology, which was a huge start. I invested in a coach who helped me to formulate my ideas and The I CAN Method was born, which you will learn about in the second half of this book.

It consists of eight weeks of empowering coaching, working one-to-one with me, where I help my client to unravel their whirring thoughts, break through their challenges and, more importantly, live their purpose. We work out how they can achieve the goals that mean something to them, no matter how large or small.

I started to share snippets of my story on LinkedIn and my social media. I explained how I used The I CAN Method to break through some of my toughest challenges in life. Before I knew it, I was getting messages in my inbox from midlife female entrepreneurs with million-pound businesses, saying how my story was resonating with them. Many asked if I could help them with their own struggles. Within 12 months I had put 15 midlife female CEOs and business founders through my empowering coaching programme.

It was lockdown, but I talked to them on video calls and it worked so well. It was amazing to see their breakthroughs— the powerful lightbulb moments that would set them free.

People were being referred to me through word of mouth, and before I knew it I had a wonderful coaching business growing that I thoroughly enjoyed, and which left me feeling fulfilled and with a purpose.

I am so proud of the fabulous testimonials on my website. I just love it so much when my clients message me to say how I have changed their life for the better. What could be better than that?

I haven't found it easy speaking in public about my life, raking through the past and opening up old wounds. In fact, when I sat down to write this book about my life story and my method, I cried. I sat with Eleanor, who came to help me write it and began by interviewing me about my life, and I wept so much I could hardly speak. The whole of that first afternoon I talked and cried, but we got there.

Everything I do, I do from the heart, whether that is this book, or my social media channels, or my public speaking. I coach with genuine empathy and understanding. There's little anyone can share with me that I haven't been through in some way. Divorce, bereavement, bankruptcy, cancer, self-doubt, rejection—I've got the t-shirt!

I talk to so many midlife, high-performing female business owners who feel lost, exhausted, overwhelmed from the constant juggle they have faced through the decades. Like me at the beginning of the pandemic, they know that if they don't do something now, it will be too late. It fills them with dread!

There are so many who need to start a new chapter, rewrite the rules so that they are at the top of their own to-do list. My method is a great starting point.

When I work with my clients, I don't tell them what to do, I don't give them the answers. The truth is that these highly intelligent women already know the answers. They just don't want to say them out loud and admit how they feel. They have been strong for so long, held it together for so long, I think it terrifies them to be vulnerable. They fear what may happen if they should open up. But as my mum would say, you can't make an omelette without breaking eggs.

I have created a safe and confidential space. I use well thought-out questions and exercises to help them gently dig out their answers and, in turn, come to their own conclusions. I urge my clients to turn their pain into power and to rip out their self-limiting roots. The point is to get to grips with the truth of their situation and to identify when that negative seed was planted that has created all those self-limiting thoughts that hold us back.

YOU are the foundation of your life, so you have to be strong to withstand the storms that can catch you off guard. If you constantly paper over the cracks without addressing the fundamental issues, one day you will disintegrate when you are put under pressure. The answer is to fix the cracks before this happens by underpinning your foundations and giving you super strength. Delving into those dark corners and cleaning them out. Really digging into and understanding those patterns will set you free.

So many influential midlife businesswomen (and because of my background, high performing equestrian types in particular) come to me for confidential coaching and support. If you were to watch these women performing their day-to-day duties, running their businesses and their homes, you would never imagine they needed support. On the outside they are strong and confident, glamorous and together—like me, they are smiling when internally they are in turmoil. I help them to break free from their struggles, to regain their self-belief and confidence so they can go on to reframe and achieve their goals. Inner peace, a stable foundation, is your strongest asset.

The I CAN Method is here to support you too.

I hope that after reading my story you are now ready to break through your challenges, be they business or personal. Just remember that you are never too old, and it is never too late to design a life you love!

You CAN do it. You ARE worth it!

Let's start on this journey together.

IGNITE YOUR
'I Can'
BREAKTHROUGH JOURNAL

THE
ICAN
METHOD™

Giving you strength to soar

WELCOME TO THE 'I Can' METHOD

Welcome to the I CAN Method™ Breakthrough Journal.

I believe that to build a business or to achieve any personal goal, you must start from a solid foundation. YOU are the foundation, you have to be secure enough to withstand any storm that may compromise you and your future plans.

My breakthrough journal supported by The I CAN Methodology is the "Strength Test" to find out how strong your foundation really is and to question is it you restricting you from realising your most meaningful goals.

The aim for you is to identify any blocks and to break down any barriers to allow you to progress forward with your future plans.

The breakthrough journal is full of thought provoking questions and exercises to encourage you to think on a deeper and broader level.

Find a quiet space where you will be uninterrupted, take your time and enjoy the process.

You are never too old, and it's never too late, to design a life you love.

With best wishes,

Sarah

THE 'I Can' METHOD

The 'I CAN' Method is my empowering mentoring programme that is designed to help you reclaim and realise your meaningful goals. You are never too old and it is never too late.

Let's get started!

IGNITE

Igniting the process, your opportunity to release the pressure valve and express how you are really feeling within a confidential environment. Reflect, Step back, look at the landscape. What is your why? Is there something holding you back? Ignite your purpose?

CLARIFY

Together we will brainstorm using a SWOT analysis, completing one on you and one on your business/goal. I will offer thought provoking questions to encourage you to think on a deeper and broader level. We will identify your key strengths and areas where you need some support or outside assistance to realise your goal.

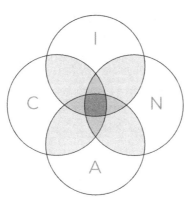

NURTURE

Create a step by step accountability list to follow, so you can nurture the process, which includes nurturing your business/goal, yourself and your own inner wellbeing to ensure you stay on track, in a position of strength.

ACTION

You will create a strategic plan following a success ladder of small steps to help you deliver your desired goal in a timely manner and without causing overwhelm. The aim is for the small goals to bring the big goal to you!

IGNITE

The first step in my 'I CAN' Method is to IGNITE your passion, your purpose and connect back with you first and then your business vision and future plans.

First you need to take a step back, stop, remove yourself from the noise and create space to think.

The matrix on a following page is to encourage you to re connect with "you" and to ignite the flame of desire so you can start building a solid foundation to realise your hopes and goals for your future.

I have created 4 Steps in this exercise. Who? When? What? and How?

I have allowed a page per question so you can really dig deep and answer with raw honesty, (you may need extra paper!).

Use the matrix, as a jotter, to note down some key words.

IGNITE

WHO?

WHEN?

WHAT?

HOW?

IGNITE - *Who*

Ask yourself who are you? Be brutally honest about who you are and how you feel.

IGNITE - *Who*

Are you happy with how things are going in your life or your business? If not why?

IGNITE - *When*

When did you last feel happy with how things were and how did happy feel?

IGNITE - *What*

What has changed to create this negative situation?

IGNITE - *What*

What can you do to change things?

IGNITE - *What*

What would be a positive outcome for you?

IGNITE - *How*

How would you like to move forward?

IGNITE - *How*

How would you like your future to look?

IGNITE - *How*

How would you feel if you achieved your goals?

CLARIFY

The second step in my 'I CAN' method is to CLARIFY your understanding of where you are now, why you are in this position and what you need to consider to get on to the right path to achieve your goals.

The matrix on the following page you will recognise as a SWOT analysis, this is to encourage you to really think about you as a whole and to identify if there are any areas of support you need in the future to help you achieve your goals.

Use the matrix, as a jotter, to note down some key words and then answer the questions in detail.

I have allowed a page per question so you can really dig deep and answer with raw honesty, (you may need extra paper!).

CLARIFY

STRENGTHS	WEAKNESSES
OPPORTUNITIES	THREATS

CLARIFY - *Strengths*

What are your strengths i.e. what are you good at?

CLARIFY - *Strengths*

What do you naturally do well without too much effort?

CLARIFY - *Strengths*

What makes you stand out from others?

CLARIFY - *Weaknesses*

Do you feel you need more support in a certain area of your life?

CLARIFY - *Weaknesses*

What weaknesses could effect your chance of success?

CLARIFY - *Weaknesses*

Which areas of your life do you feel weak?

CLARIFY - *Opportunities*

Have you ever missed an opportunity? If so Why?

CLARIFY - *Opportunities*

What opportunities would you like to explore?

CLARIFY - *Opportunities*

What opportunities are there for personal growth?

CLARIFY - *Threats*

What could stop you achieving your goals? Your main challenge or hurdle?

CLARIFY - *Threats*

How is this holding you back?

CLARIFY - *Threats*

What outside influence could threaten your route to success?

ACTION

The third step in my 'I CAN' method is to take ACTION by creating and implement a realistic plan to achieve your utopian goal.

Failing to Plan is Planning to Fail. You need an Action Plan. It is great to get things down on paper, our ideas, our hopes and our dreams, but only you can make them happen. You need a "Goal Getter Action Plan".

You may have one goal in life, you may have many, but until you put that stake in the ground and start, that goal is merely a dream.

THE SUCCESS LADDER

Your Utopian Goal is ultimately where you want to be in life or in your business. The thing that would change everything. Complete the exercises below.

What is My Utopian Goal?

What would achieving this Goal mean to me?

Achieving this Goal would give me?

I want to achieve this goal by (insert date):

How would it feel to achieve my Utopian Goal?

ACTION

Now we break this main goal down in to actionable smaller goals. Ask yourself, what are the 2-3 key things you need to do first to step onto the success ladder?

Goal 1 is to

I need to achieve this by _____ to progress my Utopian goal.

The first thing I will do to achieve this is

I completed Goal 1 on

Achieving Goal 1 has made me feel

Achieving Goal 1 has allowed me to

Goal 2 is to

I need to achieve this by _____ to progress my Utopian goal.

The first thing I will do to achieve this is

I completed Goal 2 on

Achieving Goal 2 has made me feel

Achieving Goal 2 has allowed me to

NURTURE

The fourth and final step in my 'I CAN' method is to NURTURE the process daily, which includes nurturing yourself and your own inner wellbeing to ensure you do not fall back into the negative pattern/state.

Everything in life needs some form of maintenance whether it be your car or your house, but how often do we nurture ourselves and our business?

Nurturing is taking time out to check in with ourselves or our business and to apply care and understanding and to evaluate the performance.

If we do not maintain a car it breaks down and you and your business are the same. You cannot run on empty, well you can try, but it will become ineffective and eventually not productive and fall into a negative state.

On the next page is a Nurture checklist you can use for your own PERSONAL wellbeing, there is space for you to add your own ideas based on what makes you feel energetic and ignited in your life.

You will also find a Business Nurture checklist of daily/ weekly tasks that will help you create consistency with the activities that support your business in all the areas that need to grow and flourish for sustainable success.

PERSONAL NURTURE

EACH DAY I WILL NURTURE MY PERSONAL WELLBEING BY...

☐ Start the day with gratitude and making note of all of the things I am thankful for right now.

☐ Setting out my daily action plan with my top 3 priorities.

☐ Getting up in good time to avoid the stress of having to rush.

☐ Eat healthy meals 3 times per day.

☐ Taking a lunch break to re-energise.

☐ Take 30 minutes out my day to do something I find relaxing and enjoy.

☐ Check in with family and friends.

☐ Read a book or listen to something I find inspiring.

☐ Reflecting on all the things I have achieved in the day, prior to going to bed.

☐ Creating a list of all of the things I wish to achieve the following day.

PERSONAL NURTURE

Write some of your own checklist items below

☐ ....

☐ ....

☐ ....

☐ ....

☐ ....

☐ ....

☐ ....

☐ ....

☐ ....

☐ ....

BUSINESS NURTURE

EVERY MONTH I WILL NURTURE MY BUSINESS BY...

- ☐ Reviewing my Business Stability and measuring its success against Business Plan and Forecast.

- ☐ Cash Flow - Cash is King. Are we in control of our cash? Are we getting the best deal from our bank? Are we getting the best deal from our suppliers? When did we last review our supplier agreements? Are customers paying on time?

- ☐ Systems and Processes - Are they up to date? Are they efficient? Could they be improved? Are they maximising our potential?

- ☐ Staff - Are they working productively and effectively as a team. Are they maximising their potential? Are they Happy? Have they had an appraisal?

- ☐ Customers - Are they getting a good level of service? Do I have their loyalty and do they feel fully supported by my team and I?

- ☐ Business Growth - Is my business growing year on year and are we on target? Is my marketing effective and am I getting a good return on my investment?

- ☐ Creative Thinking - By taking time out to look at the bigger picture and to engage and encourage my staff to think creatively and outside the box. To encourage staff to put forward their creative ideas and to feel a proud and valued part of the business.

- ☐ Suppliers - Am I getting the best service, price and loyalty? Do I nurture my suppliers and them me?

BUSINESS NURTURE

What is the 5 Year Plan? And is what we are doing this month working toward that?

CONGRATULATIONS!

The future is yours for the taking when you "Ignite" your passion and purpose, have Clarity on where you are and where you want to be, have an Action plan and most importantly Nurture yourself.

If you believe in yourself and follow these 4 steps, you will definitely be on the right path to turn your I CAN'TS into I CAN! and build a solid foundation for your future.

I wish you every success!

xo - *Sarah*

sarah@sarahpittendrigh.com | www.sarahpittendrigh.com

Printed in Great Britain
by Amazon

18702528R00071